PASS THAT TEST

Edited by Conor Faughnan

AA IRELAND

Gill & Macmillan
Hume Avenue, Park West, Dublin 12
with associated companies throughout the world
www.gillmacmillan.ie

© Automobile Association Developments Limited 2007
978 07171 4290 3

Text adapted by Conor Faughnan of AA Ireland from original
text by Jane Gregory
Consultant editor Noel Keeley
Designed by Jeremy Tilston of The Oak Studio Limited

Produced by AA Publishing in association with AA Ireland for
Gill & Macmillan

Traffic signs reproduced with permission of the Road Safety
Authority. © Road Safety Authority 2007

A03354

Colour reproduction by Keene Group, Andover
Printed in Italy by Printer Trento

A CIP catalogue record for this book is available from the
British Library.

5 4 3 2 1

CONTENTS

CHAPTER 3

CHAPTER 4

CHAPTER 5

INTRODUCTION

For most people, passing their driving test is an important step. It's one of the ways in which young people can show that they are growing up and becoming more responsible; like passing exams at school or college, it's an achievement to be proud of, and your pass certificate opens the gate to a whole range of new opportunities.

In this book you'll find help and advice on all the aspects of learning to drive that are covered in your practical and theory tests: the car's controls, the set exercises, legal documents, rules of the road, attitude and hazard awareness, and much more. There are other books available that give advice on particular aspects of learning to drive – none is more important than the newly re-published *Rules of the Road* which is now available from all good bookshops and from the Road Safety Authority. This book is intended to be used in conjunction with, not instead of, the *Rules of the Road*. It tells you how to apply for your theory and practical tests; what to do if you're not successful first time round; and what to look for when buying your first car. Not just for young learner drivers, it will be useful for those learning to drive later in life, or for anyone who has failed their test and wants to improve their skills ready for the next time.

It's important to know that the information you're reading is up-to-date and correct, and who better to check the facts than Ireland's motoring organisation? A team from the AA has contributed their knowledge and expertise to ensure accuracy in this book.

As a learner driver, your priorities are to acquire the skills needed for safe and competent driving through taking a course of lessons with an approved driving instructor, and to gain a thorough knowledge of your responsibilities for a lifetime of driving. *Pass That Test* is intended to reinforce and complement that learning, and provide a resource for reference between lessons and when preparing for your tests. We hope you will enjoy reading it, and find it a useful aid to learning to drive.

FOREWORD

We live in extraordinary times. Ireland's transformation since the 1990s has been astonishing. The country has grown at a phenomenal rate. Since 1990, the Irish economy has doubled in size, GDP has more than trebled, the population rose by 15 per cent and car ownership has doubled. The signs of growth surround us. The newly built motorway network, the new houses and apartments, the regeneration in the cities and towns. People have come from all over the world to live and work in a country that was once crippled by unemployment and economic stagnation.

In 2006, 173,000 private cars were registered for the first time, and over 54,000 second-hand vehicles were imported, bringing the total number of vehicles on our roads to 2.2 million. Unsurprisingly Ireland's roads have become more crowded. A careless piece of parking or casually blocking a yellow box can cause a traffic jam that will spell huge frustration for other drivers. Good driving is not really about skill. Most of us can pick up the basics of how to control a car after only a few lessons. It's more about courtesy and care: learning how to take up the correct position on the road, knowing how to react to driving situations and being helpful to other road users.

The most dangerous thing that we do every day is use the roads. In a typical year, over 350 of us will die in traffic collisions; five or six times that number will be seriously injured. The heartbreak is that every single one of those deaths and injuries is avoidable. Ireland has made so many strides in so many areas but the dreadful problem of road death still haunts us. We have not made anything like the same level of progress in improving safety on our roads. On the bright side, Ireland is now more serious than ever before about tackling this problem. There is more and better enforcement on the roads, and the Road Safety Authority is reforming the whole area of teaching and testing new drivers. But this has to begin with personal responsibility. Most people die because of simple things. When drivers go too fast for the conditions, when people don't put on seat belts, when drivers drink alcohol, they are in effect playing Russian roulette with their lives at stake.

Change is in our own hands. There are 632,000 people between the ages of 15 and 24 in Ireland. In the course of the next few years most of those young people will become car users. The coming generation of Irish drivers has an opportunity to learn better habits, to develop better skills and to adopt a better attitude than the generations that went before them.

AA Ireland is almost 100 years old. It exists to help drivers, to provide them with services and to make sure that they are treated fairly. One of its principal goals is to help to improve their safety.

I hope that this book will be helpful to you as you join the community of Ireland's motorists. It is drawn from our experience with motorists over many years, here in Ireland, through our colleagues in the UK and also through our contacts with motoring organisations and road safety experts world wide.

We owe a debt of thanks to many people who have helped us in putting the book together. Jane Gregory's original text gave us the ideal start, and we were also helped enormously by Noel Brett and Brian Farrell of the Road Safety Authority and by Michael Comer at the Department of Transport. We also had the comforting guidance of consultant editor Noel Keeley who has a wealth of experience in teaching young Irish drivers. Thanks also to Fergal Tobin and Nicki Howard of Gill & Macmillan and to Isla Love at AA Publishing.

I hope that you have a long and safe road ahead of you, and I hope that you enjoy the journey.

Conor Faughnan
AA Ireland

YOU AND YOUR VEHICLE

GET INTO THE CAR...

So – you're getting ready to go for your first driving lesson! It might help you to feel more confident if you know what to expect when you GET INTO THE CAR.

THE CONTROLS
Look around and find:
- the accelerator pedal
- the brake pedal
- the clutch pedal
- the handbrake (sometimes forgotten but very important!)
- the gear lever
- the steering wheel
- the indicators.

Check that the door is closed, then adjust your seat by moving the base backwards or forwards so that you can comfortably put your hands on the steering wheel at 'ten to two' (or 'quarter to three'), and so that you can fully depress the clutch pedal easily with your left foot. There must be at least 25cm between your chest and the centre boss of the steering wheel. The seat back should be upright in a comfortable position. Adjust your head restraint so that its top is at least as high as your eye-level. Fit your seatbelt, making sure the lap strap is well down over the hips and the

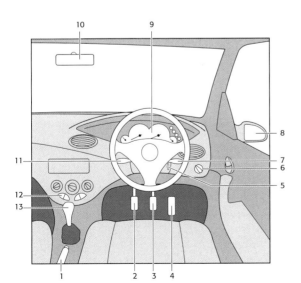

FINDING THE CONTROLS

1 handbrake
2 clutch pedal
3 brake pedal
4 accelerator pedal
5 ignition switch/steering lock
6 lighting switch
7 windscreen wiper and washer
8 side mirror
9 instuments and warning lights
10 rear view mirror
11 direction indicators and horn
12 fog lights
13 gear change lever

IIINTS & TIPS

The head restraints are there to reduce the risk of neck injuries in an accident, so make sure they are correctly adjusted.

shoulder strap clear of your neck. Then press the pedals down, making sure you can press hard on the brake without fully straightening your right leg. In the normal 'manual gearbox' car the clutch pedal will be on the left, then the brake, and the accelerator on the right. Using your left hand, go through the various gear positions. The gears control the speed of the engine relative to the car's speed. First gear is the one you select to start moving, then you change up into second, followed by third, and finally fourth gear. Most cars also have a fifth gear, which is for use on long stretches of driving at fairly high speeds. In nearly all cars the way in which you select for the four or five forward gears will be the same (see the diagram), but the position for reverse varies with different models of car – you may need to lift the lever across a 'gate', or press down and then across.

If you are going to drive an automatic car, the gear selector looks very different (see diagram below), there are only two pedals (accelerator and brake) and you control the car in a different way (see page 19).

THE INSTRUMENT PANEL

The arrangement of the dashboard will vary slightly from car to car, but there are several items that will appear somewhere on all of them.

Speedometer

Marked in kilometres / miles per hour – measures how fast you're going.

Odometer

This used to be called the mileometer, it measures how far the car has been driven. Irish cars registered in 2005 or later display odometer readings in kilometres; older vehicles almost always use miles. There may also be a trip meter, which measures the distance driven on a particular journey (useful for keeping a check on fuel consumption).

Warning (indicator) lights

For example:
- oil pressure in the engine
- brake system
- fuel level
- battery/alternator
- fasten seat belt reminder
- air bag.

Depending on the age and make of the car, other displays may be located on the panel, such as a clock. You might find the controls for the **lights** there too, but often they are located on the lever that operates the indicators.

There will be a blue light to indicate when your main **main beam** headlights are on – normally you use main beam only on roads with no street lights, and you should revert to **dipped headlights** whenever another car approaches, or when you are driving behind another car, to avoid dazzling

HINTS & TIPS

It's important to keep your headlights clean. Dirt on the glass acts as an insulator and allows heat to build up inside… this can cause a bulb to blow.

the driver. **Fog lights** have their own indicator light on the panel too; again, there are definite times for using these (see page 87). Take a few minutes to work out where all these indicator lights are – it is important to know, especially when you're driving at night.

A GOOD VIEW ALL ROUND

You also need to adjust the rear view mirror and the door mirrors to give you a good view. *Your use of the mirrors will play a key part in passing your driving test!* So make sure you can see properly in them. (See MSMM, page 18.)

Check, too, that you can see out of the car properly when driving (see adjusting your seat, page 11).

Adjust the head restraints so that they don't get in the way of your view of the traffic and of the road behind you, but are at the correct height to protect your head in the event of an accident.

The 'blind spot'

We haven't started the car yet, but now is a good time to learn about your 'blind areas'. You are sitting at the wheel with your mirrors correctly adjusted, but note that you cannot see everything in your mirrors. There is an area over your right shoulder that is not covered. Watch a cyclist or pedestrian approaching and you will see that for a moment or two they cannot be seen in any of your mirrors.

Blind areas are also caused by the door pillars and frames of your car. Get to know these now, and remember that it is critical to be aware of these areas when the car is on the move. Your driving tester will be watching how good your observation is.

SAFETY FIRST

The driving test now has a requirement for you to demonstrate a number of technical checks, and your tester will ask you how you would carry out a number of them. Quite apart from the test itself, drivers should have a basic knowledge of how to check that their car is in good shape. There are some things that you should be in the habit of checking regularly. Your car manual will have a useful list, but here are some general safety checks common to all cars:
• oil and coolant
• windscreen washer liquid
• tyre pressures and condition of tyres
• whether you need to fill up with fuel (see page 36)
• all windows are free of ice, dirt and grease

HINTS & TIPS

Don't let the oil level come higher than the upper marker on the dipstick – this could cause fouling of the spark plugs, and other problems.

• all lights and indicators working
• horn in full working order.
Many of these checks aren't just for your safety, they are *legally* necessary too.

HOW TO CARRY OUT THE CHECKS
Checking the oil

Do this when the car has been standing for several hours, and before you start the engine. Make sure the car is parked **on a level road surface** (if you're on a slope the reading won't be accurate). Pull out the dipstick and wipe with a cloth; put it back in as far as it will go, then pull it out again – the oil should come about half-way between the markers. (Some have 'Add oil' marked on the stick.) Add some engine oil if it's low, pouring it through the filler cap. If you run out of oil, the engine will seize up completely, so you should always stop the car if the oil light comes on. Some high-performance engines may require a non-standard oil – check your car's manual if you're not sure.

The engine cooling system

The liquid in the radiator is correctly referred to as 'coolant'. The scenes in days gone by of radiators boiling on hill climbs and motorists refilling them by sometimes unconventional methods aren't usually seen now, as the cooling systems in today's cars tend to be more efficient. Check your car's handbook for the correct mixture to add. If appropriate, and you need to top up the level, unscrew the coolant cap and top it up steadily. *Don't do this when the engine's hot* – you could damage both yourself and the engine.
Note: you also need to add antifreeze (see page 34).

Windscreen washer liquid

You can usually see by looking at the bottle if this needs topping up. It's best to use a proper windscreen cleaner, not just washing-up liquid which can smear the screen (see also page 35). Some screen cleaners will have an additive to help prevent the liquid from freezing on the windscreen in cold weather.

Tyre pressures

Look at your manual to find the correct pressures for the tyres. You can go to a garage or petrol station and use their equipment to check the pressures (usually this is free), or you can buy your own tyre pressure gauge. Add air if necessary to bring the tyres to the correct readings. Tyre pressures should be checked when the tyres are **cold** to ensure an accurate reading.

Check tyres for signs of wear and tear and look at the tread pattern. If the wear is uneven it could mean your wheels aren't aligned properly. Your wheels must be tracked and balanced.

Fuel

The fuel gauge will tell you if you're running low. In most cars, you get a bit of warning before you run out completely, but it's better not to risk it, especially if you're driving alone. There's also a risk of getting sediment in the engine if you run the fuel right down. (See 'All about Fuel', page 36, for what fuel to choose and how to add it – you must be aware of what fuel your vehicle uses, as mistakes can be expensive!)

HINTS & TIPS

The legal tread depth for cars is at least 1.6mm all round the tyre, across the central three-quarters of tyre width. That legal minimum is still less than ideal. The AA recommends that there is at least 3mm of tread depth to make sure there is good grip in poor conditions.

Front and rear screens

A few minutes cleaning these inside and out before your journey is time well spent, especially if you're about to drive in winter or at night. Low sun can produce glare through a greasy screen, and areas left by faulty wiper blades are a hazard in the dark. Use a clean, damp wash-leather to clean the windows.

Checking the lights

You'll need someone to stand outside the car and help you check that brake lights and indicators are working, and that the glass is clean. If you park close to a reflective surface (such as a garage door), you may be able to see for yourself if something isn't working. Sometimes you'll have to replace a bulb.

All the above need checking before setting out on a long journey; and it's good to get into the habit of **weekly checks**. Check the state of the tyres *every day*.

TEST YOUR UNDERSTANDING OF THIS SECTION

1. Where is your main blind spot?
2. What should you do if the oil light comes on and stays lit?
3. What should you check regularly on your car?
4. How do you check the oil?
5. What is the required legal depth of tread for car tyres?

ANSWERS ON PAGE 164

HINTS & TIPS

If you're parked in front of another car, or at a garage, it's often possible to look in the mirror while depressing the brake pedal, and check the lights are working in the reflection.

CAN YOU HANDLE IT?

Right then – off we go.

You'll have chosen your qualified instructor (for advice on this see 'Choosing an instructor', page 28), and you're bracing yourself to make the car move along the road for the first time – hopefully in the direction you intend.

We'll assume you're learning in an ordinary manual car. (For the starting sequence in an automatic, see page 19) Are you sitting comfortably? Can you see clearly all around? Is your seat belt fastened?

Always start the car with the gears at 'neutral'.

The handbrake should be *on*.

Wait for your instructor's signal then turn the key to *start the car*!

HINTS & TIPS

The reason you need to check over your shoulder as well as using the mirror is that there will be a blind spot just over your right shoulder, that isn't visible in the mirror.

HINTS & TIPS

You can develop cramps, muscle strains and back pains from a bad driving position. Take the time to adjust the seat carefully, making sure that you can reach all of the controls and pedals comfortably.

USING THE GEARS

Depress the clutch pedal, select first gear, and check your mirror to see if it is safe to move off. Don't forget to look over your shoulder.

Your instructor will show you how to use the clutch and the accelerator smoothly together to move off steadily.

Use your indicator if necessary before pulling out.

Then check again over your shoulder, release the handbrake and *move off*.

Move up through the gears smoothly, and down again as you approach road junctions, roundabouts or bends.

When you take your driving test, you'll need to show that you can control the car smoothly and safely.

HINTS & TIPS

The letters MSMM stand for Mirror, Signal, Mirror, Manoeuvre – it's well worth memorising this right away.

Obviously, don't pull out into the path of other motorists; and try to avoid stalling the car!

If you *do* stall – don't panic, but put the handbrake on and the gears in neutral and start the whole sequence again.

GETTING THE HABIT

Get into *good habits* from the start; put both hands on the wheel and keep them there unless you're changing gear or using the handbrake. It may look cool to cruise along with one arm resting on the window ledge, but it certainly isn't safe!

Don't drive along with your hand resting on the gear lever either.

New drivers often think they can never go as slowly as, say, a cyclist in front of them; it's good practice sometimes to see *just how slowly* you can manoeuvre – which takes us on to reversing, a routine which should *always* be done *slowly and carefully*!

REVERSING

It's important to feel just as confident about reversing as you do about normal driving. The Driving Test requires you to carry out important reversing manoeuvres in safety. These are:

• reversing round a corner
• turning in the road (see below).

The key to successful reversing is good observation of the traffic and road conditions around you, and good use of your mirrors and of the car's controls. You should also use the rear window.

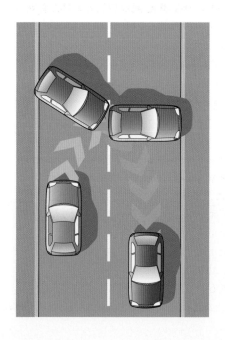

There are several places where it's not safe to reverse, for example into a busy main road, or near a children's play area. Often you can make the procedure safer by driving on a little further before you start, or even driving round the block.

For more advice on reversing, see *The Rules of the Road.*

DRIVING AN AUTOMATIC CAR

When you drive in other countries – for example, Australia or the USA – you'll find that a great many of the cars on the road are **automatics**. This means they select the appropriate gear for your speed for you as you drive.

The good news is that if you're a competent driver of a 'manual' car, you'll have very little trouble in getting used to driving an automatic. Similarly, if you go back to a manual car after driving an automatic, you'll be able to adjust without any problems.

If you take your test in an automatic you are *not qualified* to drive a manual car. So it probably makes sense, if you can, to take your test in a manual, then you're covered for any car you may later drive.

We've already looked at how the appearance and controls of an automatic car differ from a manual (see page 12); now we'll deal with start-up procedure and general driving.

Starting an automatic car

The car won't start unless the gear lever is in **Park** or **Neutral**, so check.

Then start the engine and *put your foot on the brake.*

Select **Drive** from the gears, release the handbrake and slowly lift your foot off the brake; move it to the accelerator as the car picks up speed. Use the accelerator and brake pedals with your right foot *only.*

As you pick up speed the automatic transmission will change the gears up, or change them down when you brake. Automatics are great on hills or in a line of traffic because you don't have to hold the car on the brakes and clutch. However, they do have some disadvantages; one is that they tend to use more petrol than similarly-sized manual cars.

FOUR-WHEEL DRIVE VEHICLES

Slightly different skills are needed to drive these; the manufacturer's instructions will explain how and when to select the four-wheel drive option.

TEST YOUR UNDERSTANDING OF THIS SECTION

1. What should you check before starting the engine?
2. What do the letters MSMM stand for, and what do they mean for you as a driver?
3. Why do you need to check over your shoulder as well as looking in the mirror?
4. If you take your driving test in a manual car, are you then allowed to drive an automatic transmission?
5. How do you move off when driving an automatic car?

Answers on page 164

ARE YOU LEGAL?

DOCUMENTS

Before you can get into a car and drive it on a public road you need to have the right pieces of paper to prove you're legally allowed to drive.

Theory Test

First things first: you cannot apply for a first provisional licence until you have passed the Driver Theory Test and received your certificate. This is not as daunting as the Driving test itself and with a bit of homework it is fairly straightforward.

You must make an appointment to attend one of the 41 Driver Theory Test locations throughout the country. The fee is €35.60. There you will be faced with a touch-screen multiple choice test of 40 questions on the *Rules of the Road*, and you must get at least 35 of them right to pass the test. The questions are drawn at random from a databank of 1,250 questions, and these are published in book and CD-Rom format. The book is called *The New Official Driver Theory Test – Second Edition*, and it costs €17.99.

Most people say that the 45 minutes that are allowed to answer the questions is more than enough time and that the questions themselves – once you have read the *Rules of the Road* and checked out the answers – are fairly easy. But remember to take care even with answers that seem to be very obvious. Once you receive your certificate it is valid for two years. If you let that time go by before you apply for your provisional license then you will have to go back and do the Theory Test again.

You can make a Theory Tst appointment by phone on 1890 606 106 or by text phone on 1890 616 216. You can find out more about the test on the website www.dtts.ie

Provisional licence

Everyone begins with a provisional licence (which is soon to be renamed as a Learner Permit). The licence type that allows you to drive an ordinary passenger car is called 'Category B Licence'. There are different licences for motorbikes and for larger vehicles like trucks and buses. In this book we are concentrating on the 'ordinary car' test, which is the one that is relevant for most people.

The provisional licence is normally valid for two years from the date of issue, and the fee is €15. Provided that you are at least 17 years old and do not suffer from any potentially debilitating medical condition, then you can apply to your local authority by filling out a Provisional Licence Application form (form D.201). These are available from Garda stations, motor tax offices and public libraries.

You will need a medical certificate if you do suffer from a disease or disability (or if you are over 70), and everybody must include an Eyesight Report (form D.502) when applying for their first Provisional Licence. Don't worry if you need corrective lenses to pass the Eyesight Test, but remember that if you do then you must wear them while driving.

Other rules mean that you must be normally resident in the Republic of Ireland and you must enclose either your birth certificate or your passport.

Form D.201 has a space for your photograph and signature. Take care when providing your signature – it has to be right, because it will be scanned on to both the photo licence and the paper counterpart.

You also must take care about the right sort of photo to send:
• no shadow
• not too light or dark
• no headgear
• no curtain background.

Provisional licences are not true driving licences. Despite the fact that many people in Ireland have used them for years they are simply a document that allows you to use the public roads while you are learning to drive, and as such they come with a series of restrictions. The most important of these is that Provisional Licencse holders, or 'Learner Drivers', must be accompanied by a fully licensed driver when on the road.

HINTS & TIPS

You have to produce some or all of the following documents when asked by a Garda:
• driving licence
• insurance certificate
• NCT certificate

If you can't produce them on the spot, you have to take them to a Garda station within seven days.

Your supervisor

You can't go it alone when you're learning to drive. When you're practising between lessons, without your instructor, you have to be supervised. The law states that drivers who hold provisional licences must be accompanied by a holder of a full driving licence. Remarkably, this requirement is removed for people who hold a second provisional licence but is reimposed for people who hold a third or subsequent provisional licence. This strange quirk in the law is due to be changed soon, and the new rules will stipulate that your supervisor must have at least three years' driving experience. In the meantime it certainly remains a good idea to drive accompanied until you have passed your test.

Other restrictions include that the car must display 'L' plates front and rear, and the driver is not permitted to use motorways.

All of the relevant information on provisional licenses is available on line at the Department of Transport's website, which is www.transport.ie

HINTS & TIPS

There is a legal requirement for 'L' plates to be 178mm square, with the 'L' 40 x 102 x 38mm.

Checklist for provisional licence application:

In all cases, you must enclose:
- A completed application form D.201
- Two photographs (signed on the back)
- The fee of €15
- If it is a renewal of your provisional licence, then you must include your old licence

You may also need:

- Theory Test certificate
- An eyesight/medical report
- An original birth certificate/passport
- An original certificate of registration
- Evidence that you underwent a driving test
- Evidence of a forthcoming driving test
- Lost licence declaration (Form D8.A)

Tax and insurance

All cars on public roads must display a valid tax disc and insurance disc on the windscreen. Failure to do so is an offence, and it will also mean that you fail the driving test before you even sit in the car!

The 'tax disc' is official proof that you have paid your motor tax. It is obtained from the local authority (motor tax is a major part of their funding) and it must be renewed each year. The cost varies depending on the engine size of the car; bigger engines mean bigger tax bills. A car with an engine size of less than 1 litre costs an annual €151; cars with engines larger than 3 litres cost €1,343. Others range in between. You can't drive without valid insurance that covers you for a minimum of third party liability (see 'Insurance', page 26). If you're learning with a driving school you are likely to be covered by their insurance while in the driving school car; but remember to check this with them as it is extremely important. In your own car, you need to make sure you're properly covered either with a policy in your own name or as a *named* driver on someone else's policy.

National Car Test (NCT) certificate

Cars and motor cycles have to be 'NCT'd' four years after they're first registered, and then every two years. The aim of the NCT is to check that your vehicle is mechanically safe to drive, but also that it is environmentally sound (i.e. it does not

Category of vehicle	Minimum Age	Vehicle
A1	16	Motorcycles with an engine capacity not exceeding 125cc and with a power rating not exceeding 11kW with or without sidecar.
A	18	Motorcycles with or without sidecar.
B	17	Vehicles (other than motorcycles, mopeds, work vehicles or land tractors) having a design gross vehicle weight not exceeding 3,500kg and having passenger accommodation for not more than 8 persons and where the design gross vehicle weight of the trailer is not greater than 750kg.
C	18	Vehicles (other than work vehicles or land tractors) having a design gross vehicle weight exceeding 3500kg and having passenger accommodation for not more than 8 persons and where the design gross vehicle weight of the trailer is not greater than 750kg.

C1	18	Vehicles in category C having a design gross vehicle weight not exceeding 7,500kg and where the design gross vehicle weight of the trailer is not greater than 750kg.
D	21	Vehicles having passenger accommodation for more than 8 persons and where the design gross vehicle weight of the trailer is not greater than 750kg.
D1	21	Vehicles in category D having passenger accommodation for not more than 16 persons and where the design gross vehicle weight of the trailer is not greater than 750kg.
EB	17	Combinations of vehicles with drawing vehicle in category B and where the design gross vehicle weight of the trailer is greater than 750kg.
EC1	18	Combinations of vehicles with drawing vehicle in category C1 having a combined design gross vehicle weight not exceeding 12,000kg and where the design gross vehicle weight of the trailer is greater than 750kg.
EC	18	Combinations of vehicles with drawing vehicle in category C and where the design gross vehicle weight of the trailer is greater than 750kg.
ED1	21	Combinations of vehicles with drawing vehicle in category D1 having a combined design gross vehicle weight not exceeding 12,000kg and where the design gross vehicle weight of the trailer is greater than 750kg.
ED	21	Combinations of vehicles with drawing vehicle in category D and where the design gross vehicle weight of the trailer is greater than 750kg.
M	16	Mopeds.
W	16	Work vehicles and land tractors.

'Passenger accommodation' means seating accommodation for passengers in addition to the driver.

'Design g.v.w.' means design gross vehicle weight (i.e. design laden weight). Manufacturers generally refer to it as gross vehicle weight (g.v.w.) and it is usually displayed on a metal plate attached to the vehicle by the manufacturer.

exceed the permitted levels of toxic emissions). It is illegal to drive without an NCT certificate if your vehicle should have one.

INSURANCE – LEVELS OF COVER
Third Party insurance

This is usually available as 'Third Party, Fire and Theft' cover. It's a basic insurance policy that covers you for damage to another person's car and allows you to claim on the other driver's insurance if you are involved in an accident that wasn't your fault.

Note: 'third party' means a person, or property, outside the vehicle; the 'first party' is the driver and the 'second party' the passenger.

Comprehensive insurance

This kind of policy covers damage to your vehicle even when the accident was your fault.

There are all sorts of 'catches' that apply to insurance policies, however, so – *read the small print!* You might find that some of the following apply:

Excess – This means that the insurance company won't pay, for example, the first €200 or €300 of your claim and you have to pay it yourself.

Named drivers – The insurance may only cover specific people named in the policy. You pay more if more people are covered to drive the car, and unfortunately inexperienced drivers, especially males, are proved to be higher risks and are therefore the most expensive to insure.

'No-claims' bonus. This is a feature to reward careful – and therefore cheaper in insurance terms – drivers. Typically it means a five-year scale where you get a bigger discount on your premium for each year that you stay claim free. Motorists are often reluctant to make insurance claims, especially for small amounts, in order to keep their no-claims bonus.

HINTS & TIPS

If you are involved in an accident with someone who isn't insured, or if you can't trace the person responsible, the Motor Insurance Bureau of Ireland (MRBI) has a fund for this purpose.

Policy features. Insurance policies vary, and not just in price. Some include features like Protected No Claims Discount, which would allow you one or two claims without costing you your full discount. Other features include things like free windscreen replacement. As is always the case with insurance, you need to check the details.

What about driving someone else's car?

Again, the best thing is to check the wording of the policy carefully to see whether you are covered to drive the other person's car.

TEST YOUR UNDERSTANDING OF THIS SECTION

1. What type of licence covers learning to drive?
2. How many questions must you get right in your Theory Test?
3. What does NCT stand for?
4. What is the driving licence type that covers the non-commercial driving of ordinary cars?
5. What type of road is forbidden to learner drivers?

ANSWERS ON PAGE 164

HINTS & TIPS

Useful websites:
www.transport.ie - Department of Transport
www.dtts.ie - Driver Theory Test Service
www.ncts.ie - National Car Testing Service

WHO'S IN CHARGE?

You can expect to pay up to €40 per hour for each driving lesson, so you're going to expect good value for your hard-earned cash – or, for some fortunate people, their parents' hard-earned cash!

How do you go about deciding who will teach you to drive?

You want to be sure that your driving instructor is fully qualified to teach you all the skills you need to pass your driving test.

CHOOSING AN INSTRUCTOR

Ireland is currently unique in Europe in that we have no official system for registering or monitoring driving instructors. In theory absolutely anyone – even if they have no qualifications of any kind – can operate as a driving instructor and offer driving lessons. This is likely to change soon (and it cannot come soon enough). Initially all new driving instructors will have to apply to the Road Safety Authority for accreditation, and soon thereafter the existing instructors will also need to be approved. But in the meantime the customer has no proper register to consult to make sure that their driving instructor knows what he or she is talking about.

In the absence of such a safeguard you have to be all the more careful in the research that you do. Thankfully, despite years of official neglect, Irish driving instructors are by and large a very good group of professionals who are keen to maintain high standards. Many, although not all, are part of a group called the Driving Instructor Register of Ireland. Others are likely to have other qualifications from bodies like the Institute of Advanced Motorists.

Responsibility for monitoring driving instructors has recently been given over recently to the Road Safety Authority (RSA). That body will be

> ## HINTS & TIPS
>
> Anyone, even those with no qualifications, can currently call themselves a Driving Instructor. The AA is working to change this but in the meantime remember to ask about qualifications and credentials.

HINTS & TIPS

There is more to driving than the driving test! Use your time as a learner to develop safe driving skills and hazard awareness techniques that will keep you on the straight and narrow for life.

putting in place far better rules to govern the way driving is taught in Ireland. You can learn more about them on their website, www.rsa.ie

In the meantime, before you pick an instructor you should ask for details of their qualifications. Ask them how long they have been in the job and if they have any previous students that you could contact for a recommendation. This is your money and it is for your driving education, so do not be reluctant to insist on credentials. The good instructors will not resist this, they will welcome it.

Ask around

It's a good idea to find out from your friends whether they've been impressed by a particular instructor, and which are good reliable driving schools.

That was then – this is now!

Remember, you need *up-to-date* information – so, talk to someone who has learned to drive *recently*!

Buyer beware!

Price is an important factor when choosing your driving instructor, so find out whether you can benefit from any special deals, such as a discount when you book a block of lessons in advance.

If you find a lesson price that is surprisingly low, before you decide on it, ask yourself 'WHY?'

Is there some reason why the cost is so cheap?

And don't forget to ask about the car you'll be learning in, too.
Is it modern and reliable?
Is it insured?

HOW MANY LESSONS DO I NEED?

Of course this varies from person to person, but it may be useful to know that many people need more than 30 hours of lessons.

Each lesson usually lasts one to two hours. Some driving schools offer a concentrated intensive course, but most instructors recommend learning over a period of a few months or more, backed up by practice with a supervisor. Your driving instructor will help with information about when you are ready to take the test.

A lot of good driving schools will offer a curriculum of driving tuition that goes well beyond the driving test. There are aspects like night-time driving, hazard perception and poor weather driving which are important skills to give you a solid driving education before you set out on your own. The great majority of people just think in terms of passing the test and once they have done so they never think of their lessons again. It is better to take advantage of your time as a learner to cover the ground more comprehensively; after all, you expect to be driving for your entire adult life.

Don't forget the supervisor

In addition to the driving instructor who will provide your formal lessons, you need a suitable person to supervise you when you're practising between lessons (see page 23).

TEST YOUR UNDERSTANDING OF THIS SECTION

1. What should you bear in mind when choosing a driving instructor?
2. What qualifications is an Irish driving instructor required to have?
3. In between lessons, can you drive the car on your own?
4. What documents must be displayed on a car's windscreen?
5. What should you ask about the car that you will be learning in?

ANSWERS ON PAGE 164-5

HINTS & TIPS

Useful websites:

www.rsa.ie – Road Safety Authority

www.dir.ie – Driving Instructor Register

www.irishadvancedmotorists.ie — Irish Advanced Motorists

LOOK AFTER YOUR CAR...

AND IT WILL HELP LOOK AFTER YOU!

If you want to be a good, safe driver, it makes sense to look after your car.

If your car is unreliable and lets you down it can be a real problem. You can be sure that breakdowns will never happen at a convenient time and they are extremely frustrating. More seriously, if your car is neglected or is in generally poor condition then it is more likely to develop problems that are potentially dangerous.

The car's handbook will show the recommended service intervals. Typically a car should be serviced every 16,000 kilometres, and that tends to be about once per year for the average motorist. It is important that you keep to the service schedule. If you don't then you are more likely to fail the NCT or to have a breakdown, and a full service history also maintains the value of your car if and when you choose to sell it or trade it in. Neglecting servicing can also mean expensive repair bills if something does go wrong.

Apart from the yearly service there are a few standard maintenance jobs that every driver should be able to cope with. YOU MAY BE ASKED ABOUT SOME OF THESE AS PART OF YOUR DRIVING TEST, when you are asked to demonstrate your ability to carry out a number of technical checks on your car.

Listed on the next pages are some parts of the car that will need to be checked to make sure they are in good working order.

HINTS & TIPS

The more you can learn about maintenance and the various parts of the car, the more confident you will be about checking that the person who services your car is doing a thorough job.

LIGHTS

All the lights should work, and none of them should be missing.

Check you have:
- two **main beam** headlamps
- two **dipped beam** headlamps

and that for each pair, the two lamps match each other in size and shape, and give out light of a similar intensity.

Check that the lights are angled correctly – main beam: roughly horizontal, dipped beam: angled towards the kerb (left). Give the headlights a good clean (soapy water and a soft cloth is fine), as dirt can quickly build up and reduce their effectiveness, and it can also allow heat to build up inside the lens and cause a bulb to blow.

Rear lamps

All cars must have two red lights at the back as well as the white lights at the front; again, they need cleaning, and a check to see whether the bulbs are working.

Brake lights

All cars built since 1 January 1971 must have at least **two red brake lights**.

Cars must also have **one rear fog lamp** (many have two). These are for use when visibility is poor so that traffic can see you from behind. They are powerful lights, so when conditions improve or when you are in urban traffic you should turn them off as they can be dazzling for the driver

HINTS & TIPS

The hazard warning system should work whether or not you have the engine switched on.

behind you. (See 'It's different at night', page 87 for when to use fog lamps, and when not to.)

Reflectors

Your car must have two red reflectors fitted to the back – one on each side.

Indicators

Cars must have flashing amber lights as indicators front and rear; check that these work properly.

Hazard Warning Lights

Check that when you turn on the car's hazard warning switch, all the indicator lights flash in time with each other. (See page 104 for when to use these.)

OIL

Modern cars don't get through as much oil as some older ones, but all cars use up a certain amount.

HINTS & TIPS

Dispose of used oil properly (not down the drain) – protect the environment!

Check your engine oil every 500km (300 miles) or before starting out on a long journey. (See 'Checking the oil', page 14.)

Changing the oil

This usually forms part of the car's regular service and will be done for you at the garage – it is a good idea to let them do it, as there are legal requirements about disposing of used oil.

> ### HINTS & TIPS
>
> Try to use the same type of oil each time; your car manual will have a chart that tells you which oil is best for your particular model.

> ### HINTS & TIPS
>
> Allow the engine to cool down before you open the cap! And open the cap slowly to allow the pressure to reduce slowly.

COOLANT AND ANTIFREEZE

The cooling system contains a glycol-based coolant, which protects against the effects of high and low temperatures, and also against corrosion.

While the engine's running the system is under pressure, so the temperature may sometimes rise to over 100°C – for example, if you have to wait in traffic for a while on a hot day. In modern cars this shouldn't be a

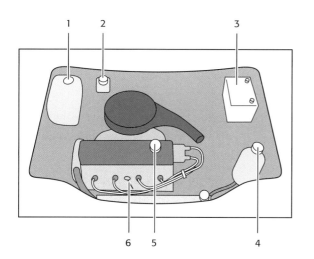

UNDER THE BONNET

1 windscreen washer reservoir
2 brake fluid reservoir
3 battery
4 cooling system reservoir
5 engine oil filler cap
6 engine oil dipstick

HINTS & TIPS

Cars with power-assisted steering are
easier to manoeuvre because the
mechanism does some of the hard work
for you. Power-assisted steering is
increasingly becoming a standard feature.

problem, but you'll need to check the
coolant level later and if necessary add
a little clean water.

Freeze protection

The coolant is designed to stay in the
system all year and should be able to
handle temperatures down to -30°C.

However, if the coolant isn't
concentrated enough, you may need to
add antifreeze. Remember what we
said earlier about 'That was then –
this is now!' Well-intentioned advice
from older motorists about adding
antifreeze may not be relevant for your
car. Ask your garage to check the
coolant concentration, and also to
recommend a good-quality antifreeze.

THE BATTERY

Again, modern cars are supplied with
the kind of sealed battery that requires
no maintenance. If your car is an older
one and *does* have a battery that needs
topping up, then you'll sometimes
need to add de-ionised water to it.

Depending on the make and type of
car, there are several more fluids to
keep a check on:
These include:
• brake fluid
• special oil for the transmission in
  automatic cars (also used for cars
  with power-assisted steering)
• screen wash fluid
• headlamp washer fluid.

BRAKE FLUID

Take care if you have any dealings
with this – it's poisonous. If it comes
into contact with your car's paintwork
it will damage it.

You can check the level of fluid in the
container; look for 'MIN' and 'MAX'
markers to indicate the correct level. If
it's below the mark, check with your
garage, because you need to find out
and deal with the cause of the
problem. (Many cars now include an
indicator light to alert you to low
levels.)

Your car manual will tell you how
often the brake fluid should be changed.

Always use new brake fluid – old fluid
is liable to deteriorate.

AUTOMATIC TRANSMISSION FLUID

It's vital that this is kept at the correct level in order for the automatic transmission to work effectively.

The oil level will be checked when the car is serviced by your garage. If you are not sure about this for any reason, then get it checked specially.

SCREEN WASH FLUID

The container for this is usually located towards one side of the engine. It's simply a case of unscrewing the cap and adding clean water, perhaps containing some screen-wash liquid.

You'll need to do this quite frequently during bad weather – and it's a legal requirement to keep it topped up. While you're driving behind any large vehicle in rain, or when there's mud on the road, spray from the vehicle in front can coat your screen with particles, and if there's a low sun in front as well you will very quickly find you can't see anything unless you can clear your screen.

You can get similar problems in fine summer weather but this time it's caused by small insects (bugs) sticking to the windscreen!

HINTS & TIPS

Wear protective gloves when handling any of these fluids.

In freezing weather the screen-wash mechanism won't work and you run the risk of water freezing on the windscreen; clean ice off all glass surfaces *before* you start driving (see 'Stormy weather', page 88) and use a proper winter-grade additive in the screen wash.

HEADLIGHT WASHER FLUID

Some cars are fitted with a headlamp washer system. Again, look for the filler cap in the engine compartment.

WINDSCREEN WIPERS

You need to keep the wipers in good working order. A damaged wiper blade will fail to clear the screen properly, and leave smears or arcs of dirt, making it dangerous to drive because your field of vision is reduced. It will also mean an NCT failure.

You can clean the blades with a soft cloth, but you may need to replace them if they've become hardened or cracked – maybe as a result of being frozen to the screen, or being exposed to heat, salt or the wrong sort of cleaning agent.

How to change the blades

- Turn off the ignition when the wipers are in the upright position.
- Lift up the wiper arm slightly.
- Use the release mechanism to remove the damaged blade.
- Replace with a new one.

SEAT BELTS

Make sure that these are in good working order, then keep an eye on them for signs of wear, non-functioning mechanisms etc.

The seat belts will be checked as part of the NCT.

Modern cars have seat belts for the driver and every passenger. The law says that you must wear your seat belt, and the driver is also legally responsible for the belts of all passengers under the age of 17. It should become an automatic habit for all drivers to wear seat belts at all times. Not only is it the law, it makes a dramatic difference to your safety if you are involved in a crash.

> **HINTS & TIPS**
>
> Avoid getting seat belts twisted, as this can add to injuries in an accident. Always replace seat belts after an accident.

> **HINTS & TIPS**
>
> Where there are seat belts fitted they must be worn, except in the case of people holding an exemption certificate for medical reasons.

Unless you've got a much older car, your seat belts will be of the inertia reel kind which extend to fit the passenger. The older static belts have to be adjusted manually.

See 'It's your responsibility' (page 127) for what you need to know about passengers and seat belt law.

ALL ABOUT FUEL

The main things to be aware of here are:

- taking care you don't run out
- using the right kind
- knowing how to operate a petrol pump.

How much fuel in the tank?

Remember to check the fuel gauge before you set out (see page 15 for a reminder of why this is important).

If your fuel gauge doesn't work – *GET IT SEEN TO!*

It's not a good idea (because of fire risk) to carry a full can of fuel in the car in case of emergency; but you *could* sensibly carry an empty can, so that you could walk to a garage.

Which type of fuel?

Although there are alternative fuels, almost all cars on the road use either petrol or diesel. Which fuel you use doesn't really make any difference from the point of view of the driver, but it obviously makes a big difference to the engine so you have to use the right one!

Petrol and diesel pumps are clearly marked and the nozzle widths are also different which in theory should make it impossible to put diesel into your petrol tank by mistake. Impossible or not, it does happen. The AA comes across nearly 700 cases per year on average. This can mean an expensive repair bill, so needless to say you should take care to avoid it.

See 'Putting fuel in the car' on page 38.

HINTS & TIPS

Catalytic convertors and unleaded petrol between them have reduced harmful emissions from cars by over 90 per cent since the early 1990s. But burning fuel still produces CO_2, which is a greenhouse gas.

CATALYTIC CONVERTERS

Unless you have a car that was built before 1992, petrol models will be fitted with a catalytic converter. A *catalyst* means something that enables a chemical change to take place; the catalytic converter, which is located in the car's exhaust system, converts pollutant gases into less harmful gases.

Owning a car fitted with a *catalytic converter* **should encourage you to drive even more carefully**. This is because they are fairly easily damaged – for example, if you were to back the car into a wall and hit the exhaust pipe or if unburnt fuel enters the converter, or if you drive through deep water or deep snow.

Unburnt fuel can enter the converter if you:
• repeatedly turn the starter key because the engine is cold, thus 'flooding the engine'
• 'bump-start' the car, by pushing or towing.

Try to avoid these situations by:
• making sure as many electrical components as possible are turned off when you're starting up: eg, lights, radio, front and rear window heaters, fans. Once the engine is running you can switch on those you need.

• instead of bump-starting, use **jump-leads** to start the car by linking up to another car battery.

Diesel engines do not have catalytic convertors. Diesels typically produce better fuel economy but may not have quite the same power as petrol engines, although this is not quite as true as it used to be with modern diesel technology. You should never allow your car to run out of fuel while driving, if you can avoid it, and this is particularly true with diesels.

PUTTING FUEL IN THE CAR

It can be quite alarming to find, once you're the proud possessor of a 'pass' certificate, that you haven't a clue how to put fuel in your car!

So, here's a useful list of reminders for YOUR FIRST TRIP TO THE GARAGE.

• Have you got cash, or a credit or debit card, to pay for the fuel?
It's all too easy to fill the car up and then find you've forgotten your wallet.

HINTS & TIPS

You could ask your driving instructor to accompany you to a filling station in the course of your lessons.

• Which side of the car is your filler cap? Once you've sorted this out, then you'll know which side of the pump to park at the garage.
• How does your car's filler cap open? It helps to know this before you arrive at the garage. In most cars it unlocks with a key, and sometimes there is also a release lever inside the car.
• As soon as you have parked in the correct position at the garage, switch off your engine – this is very important, as fuel and the fumes from it are highly combustible.
• For the same reason – don't smoke!
• You'll see a row of pumps with the fuel descriptions written on them, and also coloured caps to help you further. The pump with the green cap will be the one for unleaded fuel. The diesel pump may be black or grey. There may be other variations, e.g. 'Super Plus Unleaded'; if you're in any doubt, ask for advice, or check your car manual.
• Remove the filler cap.
• Lift the fuel dispenser from the pump and place it into your tank as far as it will go.
• Check that the display on the pump is at zero.
• Squeeze the trigger and carry on filling until you have as much as you need. If you fill the tank full you will

HINTS & TIPS

Most garages in Ireland are self-service, but when travelling in some other parts of the world you may have your car filled up by an attendant.

feel the pump handle click in your hand as it cuts off automatically. Don't attempt to fill the tank any further after this.

- Replace the fuel dispenser and the filler cap.
- Use a piece of the paper towel roll provided to wipe off any fuel around the fuel inlet (or from your own hands or feet).
- Note the number of the pump you used, and then go and pay, and drive away. Some pumps will accept credit and debit cards.
- Do not use a mobile phone on the garage forecourt as this can interfere with the controls of the pumps.

HINTS & TIPS

Alternative fuels like Ethanol E85 and biodiesel can be used – after some modifications to the car – instead of ordinary fuel. Because they are made from biomass rather than fossil fuels they do not increase the amount of CO_2 in the atmosphere.

ENVIRONMENTALLY FRIENDLY

You'll know that as well as using unleaded fuel, one way to keep your motoring as 'green' as possible is to aim for maximum fuel efficiency.

There are several ways to achieve this:
- Have your car serviced regularly by a reliable garage. Correct engine tuning is a must to keep fuel use and emissions to a minimum.
- Keep your tyres at the right pressures – driving on under-inflated tyres uses up more fuel.
- Avoid harsh acceleration.
- Don't drive too fast – speed increases fuel consumption. But do drive in the highest possible gear for the speed you're driving at.
- Don't leave a roof rack on the car when you don't need one; roof racks cause 'drag' and make the car less aerodynamic.
- The air conditioning system, and especially 'climate control' systems, are actually very thirsty features. Using them excessively can add as much as 10 per cent to your fuel usage.
- Try to plan journeys to avoid crawling through traffic for long periods – use public transport, or even go by bike!

YOU AND YOUR VEHICLE

ALTERNATIVE FUELS

We are beginning to see the use of
alternative fuels in Ireland, and with
global issues like climate change and
the cost of oil becoming ever more
important, this trend is likely to
continue.

Although there are many different
kinds, the two main fuels are ethanol
(called E85 as it contains 15% petrol),
which is used as a substitute for
unleaded petrol, and Biodiesel, which
as the name suggests is used in place
of diesel. Cars need to be modified to
use these fuels, but they are becoming
an increasingly popular and
environmentally friendly option.

HINTS & TIPS

The size of the fuel inlet on newer cars is
quite small, to match the diameter of the
pump dispenser for unleaded petrol;
sometimes you'll find a reminder printed
near the fuel inlet on the car, 'Unleaded
Fuel Only'.

TEST YOUR UNDERSTANDING OF THIS SECTION

1. Why should you get your car serviced regularly?
2. Why should you be careful to turn off your fog lights once visibility improves?
3. Brake fluid needs to be handled with care. Why?
4. What is meant by power-assisted steering?
5. Why is it dangerous to drive when your windscreen washer fluid container is empty?
6. Are passengers travelling in the rear of your car legally required to wear seat belts?
7. What is the purpose of a catalytic converter?
8. What safety precautions should you observe when visiting a garage to fill up with fuel?
9. At a service station, how do you know when your fuel tank is full?
10. In what ways can you do your best to be a 'green' motorist?

ANSWERS ON PAGE 165

ON THE ROAD

MOTORISTS WITH ATTITUDE

While you're learning to drive, you'll probably hear a good deal about the virtues of *defensive driving*. This means anticipating hazards, being aware of what other motorists and pedestrians may do, and avoiding taking risks.

Often people who have just passed their test and are raring to go aren't too keen on being told to adopt a cautious approach at all times.

Think about how you would respond to these two statements:
• I aim to be a careful and safety-conscious driver.
• I intend to be a fast and skilful driver.

To many young drivers, the second one sounds a whole lot more appealing than the first. It doesn't help that the word 'courtesy' almost always comes after the word 'old-fashioned'!

HINTS & TIPS

Almost 30% of all the drivers killed on the roads are between the ages of 18 and 24. In this category, male deaths outnumber females by a ratio of 4:1. (Source NRA)

Research has shown that young drivers tend not to develop the ability to anticipate hazards successfully until they are older and more experienced (see 'Hazard awareness', page 48). Driving instructors aim to teach some hazard awareness skills, and questions on this form part of the **Theory Test**. But there is no substitute for experience. Every piece of research available shows that the younger and less experienced a driver is, the more likely they are to have an accident. Whether we like it or not, it is also true that young males are at far greater risk.

WHY ARE YOUNG DRIVERS MORE AT RISK?

Passing your driving test seems to have become something of an initiation ritual in our society, especially for males; it's as if getting through the test is part of becoming an adult. Maybe that's why getting your licence can be followed by an urge to drive too fast and 'show off' to passengers and other drivers. It is also natural to enjoy the freedom and independence of being a driver.

Learning the mechanical skills of driving a car is relatively easy. Most of us can get the hang of it after only a few lessons. Young men tend to respond to a physical challenge and to enjoy the act of driving, and in fact in terms of the physical skill and dexterity needed young men tend to be very good. In fact young people have faster reaction times than older people, which you would think would be an advantage on the road. But there is a great deal more to good driving than learning how to control the car.

The real skill is in anticipation, hazard awareness and making sensible choices. If a young man takes a corner too fast and brilliantly controls the car when it starts to slide, bringing it expertly back under control, then he has demonstrated that he is an appalling driver. He may have the reflexes of a fighter pilot, but he has the judgement of a fool. The truly skilled driver is the one who took the corner at a smooth, gentle and appropriate speed at which there was never any danger.

Therefore, if you don't want to end up as 'just another statistic', having a positive approach to road safety *is the only way to go.*

A CAR IS NOT AN OFFENSIVE WEAPON

This sounds obvious; but drivers will often subconsciously see their car as an extension of themselves, and the way they drive as an expression of their personality. There are drivers who react angrily when another car cuts in front of them. There are those who think that being overtaken is some sort of personal insult, as if being the car behind is in some way an inferior position.

Of course when you think about this rationally you realise that it is ridiculous, but driving is one of those situations where we can tend to react irrationally. It is an instinct in many of us which the good driver has learned to control.

A lot of the social stereotypes glorify and reinforce bad driving. Think of the hundreds of films that have been made in which reckless car chases are shown as dangerous but glamorous.

HINTS & TIPS

Fatalities make headlines, but for everyone killed on the roads a further six are seriously injured.

A car is rather more than just a means of getting from A to B. It is a substantial investment, and usually it is a prized possession. Owners take pride in their cars and enjoy driving them. The trick is to keep that pride in perspective and not let it show itself in reckless, risky driving. This gives you a much better chance of keeping your pride and joy – not to mention your body – in one piece.

Road rage

The AA has carried out extensive research into what makes people engage in road rage. Some of the reasons put forward to explain it are:

- frustration at being kept waiting in traffic congestion
- aggravation if your most cherished possession – your car – has been, or is at risk of being, damaged
- noise: the din of surrounding vehicles, and car radios, can lead to stress and aggression
- hot weather: high temperatures, at times of the year when holiday jams can occur, do seem to make matters worse!

If you are the type of person who finds these situations stressful or annoying, then you need to be conscious of the fact that you might be prone to 'road rage'.

ATTITUDES TO SPEED

Very often, drivers' attitude problems are about *their attitude to speed limits*.

Problems arise when people drive at a speed which is *inappropriate* for the conditions – type of road, visibility and weather, etc.

It's amazing but some people think:
- that speed limits are only meant for people with poor reaction times
- that 'no overtaking' regulations are only meant for people with less powerful cars
- that you can break the speed limit while you are overtaking
- that speed limits are not maximum speeds but recommended cruising speeds.

Attitudes such as these explain why avoidable crashes still happen.

CHAPTER 2

Speed on the open road

You may notice that you're tempted to allow other drivers to dictate the speed at which you drive when you're on the road. It can be easy to speed up when there is a car behind you, or to just follow the car in front without realising that you are both speeding. Every driver on the road knows, or ought to know, that they should not exceed the speed limit, but unfortunately a lot of people take a cavalier attitude to limits. According to NRA research (Survey of Free Speeds 2006) 28 per cent of drivers exceed the speed limit on dual carriageways. Small wonder that the road safety figures in Ireland are so poor.

Correct driving means taking a position on the road which is well back from the car in front. You should always be able to stop your vehicle within the distance that you can see ahead of you to be clear. When following another vehicle, remember the 'two second rule'. Watch the car in front as it passes a mark that you can take note of – for example a signpost or a road marking. You should be able to say the phrase 'only a fool breaks the two second rule' before your car reaches the same point. This is a well known rule and you may be asked about it by your driving tester.

Also remember that the two second rule applies in good driving conditions. On wet roads your braking distances increase greatly – and so should your caution. **Keep your distance**; it can literally be a matter of life and death. Not to mention failing your driving test!

Speed and your passengers

Research carried out in the UK* shows that the presence of a young male *passenger* will have an effect on the speed of the *driver*. He or she will drive faster than usual. Passengers, on the other hand, generally wish the driver would slow down!

Don't make the same mistake again

It also seems that people don't learn from experience:
- drivers are often involved in the same kind of accident twice.

So – if you're unlucky enough to have an accident, or even a 'near-miss', try to ask yourself *what you can learn* from the experience to help prevent the same type of accident happening next time.

Frank McKenna, Department of Psychology, University of Reading

WHAT CAUSES ROAD ACCIDENTS TO HAPPEN?

Firstly, road safety experts don't refer to 'accidents' any more. The word implies something that couldn't be avoided, whereas a car crash is almost always down to a human mistake.

- 95% of crashes are caused by **people** – not by mechanical or other problems.

Some of the most frequent causes of accidents are:
- the driver losing control of the car
- the driver losing concentration
- cars crossing the path of other vehicles
- rear-end shunts.

You're less likely to have an accident if you:
- drive at an appropriate speed, keeping full control of the car
- don't follow so closely behind the car in front that you can't stop if necessary to avoid running into the back of it
- don't overtake and then 'cut in' on other drivers.

We'll look in more detail at driving behaviour in Chapter 3.

TEST YOUR UNDERSTANDING OF THIS SECTION

1. Who has the fastest reaction time – young motorists or older people?
2. What is the best speed to drive at?
3. What percentage of crashes are caused by human error?
4. Should you 'coast' downhill to save fuel?
5. What is the 'two-second rule', and what does it mean?

ANSWERS ON PAGE 165–6

CHAPTER 2

HINTS & TIPS

You should avoid getting into the habit of coasting, or letting the car run downhill in neutral. This leads to loss of control of your braking.

I DIDN'T EVEN SEE HIM...

HAZARD AWARENESS

How often does a motorist protest that the accident happened before they had time to realise the person they hit was there?

Much research has been done internationally which shows that the driving skill of *anticipation* is one that only comes with experience. Young people are not necessarily bad at judging traffic situations, but they do lack experience. Noticing potential hazards before they develop is a critical part of being a good driver. How can a young driver make up for this? More to the point, how can you convince a driving tester that you are safety conscious and aware of potential danger?

Firstly, slow down. Your tester will want to see a smooth and controlled drive, with your speed matched to traffic conditions. You will have to demonstrate that you are observing correctly, that you are using your mirrors and that you have positioned your car and managed your speed in such a way that you will be able to react in time to any incident that arises. What if a child ran out in front of you right now? If you are driving properly then you will have time to control the car and stop safely. If you are over-confident, if you are not concentrating and certainly if you are going too fast, then even your fighter-pilot reflexes won't prevent a disaster.

ANTICIPATION

Accidents do not just happen. They come about because of preventable mistakes that people make. Human beings are not robots and mistakes will occur. Part of your instructor's job while teaching you to drive is to help you learn to anticipate problems before they happen.

Anticipation involves:
- noticing what's happening around you while you're driving
- anticipating what you might expect to happen next
- deciding what you should do about it.

HINTS & TIPS

As well as the hazards described here, always expect the unexpected!

HINTS & TIPS

Roads are more dangerous at night. Nearly 15% of all fatal car crashes happen between midnight and 6am, despite low traffic volumes at those hours. Sadly the death of young people in single vehicle crashes at night is a regular feature of Ireland's roads.

Anticipation is one of the **key skills** you need to be a safe driver, in addition to:
• observation
• concentration
and
• forward planning.

OBSERVATION

For drivers, *this means more than just looking.*

It should involve *all* your senses; you might *hear* a hedge cutter just around the corner, or smell grass being cut.

It means *looking for information.*

Train yourself to scan as much of the road as you can in your field of vision, to give you more time to decide what action to take if you see a **hazard** coming up.

On the look-out for hazards

Think about the times and places where you're most likely to run into hazards on the road; such as the rush hour, or the end of the school day.

Times to take even more care than usual of course include driving in bad weather or at night; but you're also at risk when you have to *slow down suddenly, or make a right or left turn* at a junction where you can't see clearly all around.

Areas to be particularly careful are:
• where there are parked vehicles
• around pedestrian crossings
• at roundabouts and junctions
• near entrances to schools
• Areas where there are likely to be children about.

Parked vehicles

Watch out for:
• a child suddenly running out between parked cars. (Is there an ice-cream van on the opposite side of the road? Are there children playing on the path? Is there an entrance to a park or sports field?)
• a cyclist riding close to the parked cars – you may have to pull out further to overtake them
• car doors opening into the road space
• cars pulling out from the parked lines.

CHAPTER 2

Pedestrian crossings

Get to know the different types of
pedestrian crossings; you'll need this
information in your driving test.
(See also page 66.)

When approaching a zebra crossing –
slow down and be prepared to stop.
At pelican, puffin and toucan
crossings –
• *stop* if the lights are red
• *give way to pedestrians* if the amber
  lights are flashing
• *give way to cyclists* on a toucan
  crossing.

Roundabouts and junctions

Anticipation plays a big part here, as
you have to position your car correctly
in advance.

Get in the appropriate *lane* (if there
are lanes) in good time, and *slow
down* enough to be able to make the
turn in a safe and controlled manner.
(See 'It's in the rules', pages 63–5, for
more on lanes and roundabouts.)

Motorcycles

Motorcycles are another possible
hazard to be aware of.

Like bicycles, they can be blown off
course in high winds, and sometimes
they're surprisingly difficult to see.

Also, check your door mirrors on both
sides for motorcycles filtering between
lanes in queues of traffic. Do not
forget your blind spots. You should
not change lanes without checking
over your right shoulder.

At some angles, even a lamp post can
hide a motorcyclist.

Cyclists and horse riders

You need to exercise caution when
behind a cyclist near a junction or
roundabout; it's safest not to overtake,
but to stay behind them, as they may
change lanes unexpectedly.

Cyclists are more at risk than car
drivers when there are strong winds,
and could be blown off course. They
may also have to swerve to avoid

things like drain covers or potholes at the side of the road. If the door of a parked car opens the cyclist may swerve out unexpectedly – are you ready? Give them plenty of room.

Keep a good distance between your car and anyone riding a horse; avoid revving the engine as you overtake! Remember, too, to anticipate that they might be ahead of you and out of your field of vision on narrow country lanes; slow down, and be prepared to stop.

CONCENTRATION

You can't afford to let your concentration slip even for a moment when you're driving. At high speeds, the total distance you need to see the hazard, brake and come to a stop can be as much as 107.5 metres (or 24 car lengths) – that's at 120kph. (See 'Stopping distances', page 74.)

So if you weren't *fully awake*, or if you were *distracted* for some reason, you might fail to stop in time.

HINTS & TIPS
Don't forget – MSMM, and remember your blind spot!

HINTS & TIPS
Don't forget – you may have to deal with more than one hazard at a time!

You can be distracted by many things, including:
• roadside distractions
• passengers
• pets
• information overload
• mobile phones.

Roadside distractions
These include eye-catching posters; pedestrians who attract your attention for some reason; and (least excusable) turning to look at the scene of an accident as you drive past.

Passengers
Passengers can distract you by sudden movements or incessant talk – all parents have different approaches to controlling their children while in the car, and different views on how much noise they can tolerate on a scale from zero to bedlam. It's important to have children strapped securely into a child seat, or the back seat for older children. (See 'It's your responsibility', page 127.)

Pets

As with children, it's just as important to convey animals properly in the car, so that they don't distract you. A harness designed to be fastened through the seat belt is available for dogs.

Information overload

Compared with someone learning to drive 20 or 30 years ago, you now have so much more to watch all at once.

Road signs, traffic hazards such as lanes merging, or roadworks, all compete for your attention and demand constant decision-making.

It's not surprising that people cope by being *selective* about the information – focusing on some things at the expense of others.

MOBILE PHONES

Mobiles are a relatively recent technology. It is only in the last decade or so that they have become universal. It is worth noting that they are lifesavers, and in fact the AA recommends that you have a mobile phone with you in the car. They are by far the fastest way to contact the emergency services if you need them, and they are also the best way to call for help if you have a breakdown. Your personal safety is important, and rather depressingly this is an area where females can feel particularly threatened. The mobile means you can call for help without leaving the car.

However, mobiles phones are an absolute scourge when you are actually driving. You should never answer the phone while driving. There is just no such thing as a call that is so urgent that you cannot take a few moments to pull in safely before dealing with it. Modern phones will log the caller's number or take a message, so you can get back to them in a few minutes. Can you honestly say that you need to answer the phone immediately? Put it on silent, or better still turn it off, and deal with any messages after you have parked.

It has taken a few years for the research and the law to catch up with the technology, and there are still people out there who will swear that the phone is no problem – after all, you are allowed talk to passengers. However it is now proved that phone use is severely distracting, much more so than talking to passengers or listening to the radio. Why?

When you talk to someone a great deal of the communication between you is non-verbal. Smiles, eye contact, hand gestures – these are a natural part of a conversation. On the phone you don't have these, and the brain compensates. It's called cognitive impairment.

Consider how you behave on the phone when you are not driving. You might wander into the kitchen and out again or walk up and down the room without thinking about it. When you hang up you wonder where you left your cup of coffee. This type of distraction is potentially lethal while driving, and the facts bear this out.

Research proves you are four times more likely to be involved in an accident if using a mobile phone while driving.

Experienced drivers are no better. Tests show that they suffer the same level of distraction and are just as likely to make errors while using a phone as inexperienced drivers, nor is there any significant difference between the sexes.

Like most developed countries, Ireland now has a law which makes it illegal to use a hand-held phone while driving. While hands free devices remain legal the AA advises that you do not use them unless it is absolutely necessary and never get involved in a detailed conversation while on the move.

THE ANSWER'S SIMPLE! – find a safe place to stop and *then* make the call.

CHAPTER 2

FORWARD PLANNING

This is the skill that you need so that you can act on what you have observed on the road ahead.

For example:

You're coming up to a roundabout and you can see that traffic is stationary on the opposite side. By looking ahead you can work out that if you move on to the roundabout, you will block other traffic from flowing and leaving at other exits. So, after **observing** the situation you would use your **forward planning** skills to avoid making the problem worse.

You might also see that there is an incident up ahead. Perhaps a lane is blocked because of roadworks or a minor collision. This might mean that the right turn that you were going to take will mean that you block the road entirely, so in consideration for other road users you drive on and use a different route.

> ### HINTS & TIPS
>
> Motorway driving is where you need your forward planning skills most of all; in deciding when to overtake, signalling and moving out in good time, and anticipating hazards ahead. (See also Motorway rules, page 92.)

> ### HINTS & TIPS
>
> Make sure the car's ventilator fans are working efficiently, and do not set the temperature too high. This will help you stay alert, but it does not take the place of taking a proper rest.

Summary

All of these key skills work together to make you a better driver.

- If you're *concentrating* on the road
- And *observing* what's happening
- You'll be able to *anticipate* possible hazards
- And *plan* your actions ahead.

ALERTNESS

There's another reason why you might not spot an approaching hazard until you're almost on top of it – it could be summed up like this:

ARE YOU FIT TO DRIVE?

'Fit' can mean:

- Have you had any alcoholic drinks before you set out?
- Are you under the influence of illegal substances (drugs)?
- Are you feeling groggy or unwell?
- Are you taking prescription medicine which could affect your ability to control the car?
- Are you too tired to drive?

CHAPTER 2

We'll deal with drink and drugs a little later (see 'Driving under the influence', page 82).

It's unwise to set out on a journey if you're not well, on the basis of 'I'll see how I go – I'll probably be all right':
• your reactions are likely to be *slower*
• you may be *unable to judge* distances properly
• your actions may be *less well co-ordinated* than usual.

And of course, warnings printed on the labels of prescription medicines such as
'DO NOT DRIVE OR OPERATE MACHINERY' are put there for good reasons!

Driver Fatigue

Driver fatigue is one of our major killers. It is up there with drink-driving, not wearing seat belts and speeding. In fact the Road Safety Authority published research recently that showed that as many as 20% of driver deaths in Ireland may have been caused by fatigue.

HINTS & TIPS

If you doze off for five seconds when travelling at 100kph that means you will travel over 130 metres 'blind'.

If you are tired and there is some distance to go to a service station, open the window for a few moments to let in some fresh air. But remember: this does not stop tiredness affecting your driving.

If you drive when you are too tired you risk falling asleep at the wheel. Even if you do not literally doze off you will find that you are succumbing to 'micro-sleep' where you drift out of consciousness for a few seconds at a time even with your eyes open. Driving for long stretches on a motorway at night can be especially dangerous. If you sense that you are losing your concentration, then take a break. Make use of motorway service stations to stop for a caffeine drink and a short walk before resuming your journey.

Plan your journey ahead, giving yourself plenty of time for rest stops – at least every couple of hours. Avoid having a heavy meal before setting off. Fatigue-related crashes are most likely to occur at night but another high-risk time is between 2pm and 6pm in the afternoon when our body clocks are naturally low. To end this section, here are some of the hazards you're likely to encounter in everyday driving, and how you might deal with them.

Hazard

A slow vehicle such as a milk float or road maintenance vehicle is going up a steep hill in front of you.

Response

You can overtake, but only if:

- you can see it's safe to do so
- there are no road markings or signs prohibiting overtaking
- the road is sufficiently wide
- you have scanned for pedestrians.

Hazard

There are parked vehicles on your side of the road – not leaving enough room for two cars to pass.

Response

Give way to traffic from the other direction.

Stop well behind the parked cars so that you can see clearly to move out when it's your turn.

Hazard

A bus starts to pull out in front of you and you can only allow it to do so if you slam on your brakes.

HINTS & TIPS

Don't forget to watch out for pedestrians (especially children) appearing from between the cars (see page 49).

Response

If driving along a road where buses operate, anticipate that they may need to pull out and allow them to do so. If you have to slam on your brakes to let the bus pull out, you're already going too fast.

Hazard

The roads are icy, and it's foggy too.

Response

You need to adapt your normal driving technique to minimise the risk of accidents. Allow as much as ten times the normal distance between you and the car in front. And decide whether your journey is really necessary.

Hazard

You notice that there are tram rails on the road.

Response

Keep a sharp look out for trams – they may approach silently, and cannot steer out of the way to avoid a motorist.

Hazard

You come across a set of road works.

Response

Slow down. If the road works require you to change lanes, remember to indicate and check your blind spot. Be conscious of the fact that there are workmen present and that there may be a danger to them. Be aware that the road surface may be slippery and that there may be loose chippings.

There are innumerable other hazards we could list here; they can involve unusually large or slow vehicles, extreme weather conditions, and obstructions of one kind or another. Your driving tester will be watching to see how you cope with them, and whether you are anticipating any potential hazards.

Once you've passed your test, it's very trying to find that some other drivers don't obey the same rules:

• for example, if you've kept a good distance between you and the lorry in front so that you can see clearly to overtake, and then someone overtakes you and fills the gap!

But stick with the driving techniques that you know to be right; don't be tempted to behave badly because others are doing so.

REMEMBER – YOU ARE DRIVING WITH THE AIM OF REACHING YOUR DESTINATION SAFELY; YOU ARE NOT IN COMPETITION WITH OTHER DRIVERS.

TEST YOUR UNDERSTANDING OF THIS SECTION

1. What are some of the key skills you need to be a safe driver?
2. What things can distract you from concentrating on your driving?
3. What should you do if you need to make a call on your mobile phone when you're driving?
4. If the journey to your holiday destination takes about six hours, how many rest stops should you make along the way?
5. When driving in icy conditions, you need to allow extra space between you and the car in front. Is it: twice the normal distance, four times, or ten times?

ANSWERS ON PAGE 166

CHAPTER 2

HINTS & TIPS

In bad conditions you need to double and treble the amount of care that you take. Slow down, keep a safe distance and expect the unexpected.

IT'S IN THE RULES

The most complete guide to the rules for drivers is, of course, the *Rules of the Road*. This is a comprehensive document which has been fully updated and is available from the Road Safety Authority. Everyone who drives on an Irish road should be aware of that document and should know its contents. It is an essential part of learning how to drive.

In it you'll find rules not just for motorists but for pedestrians, cyclists and motorcyclists as well; and rules for horses, dogs and other animals on the road.

You'll need to study the *Rules of the Road* as part of your preparation for both the Theory Test and the Driving Test itself. And when you take your practical test, the driving tester will assess your knowledge of the *Rules of the Road* from your general driving.

What follows is a summary of some of the rules relating to:
- **crossroads**
- **junctions**
- **lanes and roundabouts**
- **pedestrian crossings and level crossings**
- **road signs and road markings**
- **speed limits**
- **stopping distances.**

A separate section focuses on parking, and another on motorway rules.

(*Note:* traffic signs used on motorways will be dealt with in the 'Motorway Rules' section, page 92.)

CROSSROADS

At a crossroads you'll find some of the following:

- a roundabout
- traffic lights
- road signs
- road markings (see diagrams below)
- nothing at all! (see diagram right)

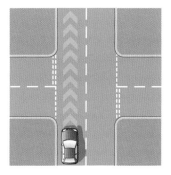

Fortunately, the last one is becoming increasingly rare, but where you do find an unmarked crossroads, it's one of the places where there is a *high risk of accidents*.

At an unmarked crossroads – *no one has priority*.

So, look all around and take care before proceeding.

There are certain conventions (which people don't always observe), such as:

- If you're going straight across and there's someone opposite who wants to turn right, generally you go first.
- If you're both waiting to turn right, you're supposed to drive around each other right side to right side.

However, it's not against the law to go left side to left side – but it is more risky, as your view of oncoming vehicles will be blocked.

HINTS & TIPS

Junctions are dangerous, leaving drivers vulnerable to the 'T-bone' type collision where one car strikes another on the side. These crashes are often fatal.

CROSSROADS WITH TRAFFIC LIGHTS

Make sure you're quite clear on:
- the meaning of all the traffic light signals
- the sequence of colours.

Green means 'Go' – *but only if you can see that it's safe.*

Amber on its own means 'Stop'. It is illegal to drive through an amber light unless you are so close to the signal when it changes that stopping would be dangerous.

Red means 'Stop'

> ## HINTS & TIPS
>
> Traffic lights don't always work. If you come to a set that are broken, take extreme caution and obey the rules that apply to crossroads or T junctions, whichever is relevant.

If you can see that the road beyond the lights is still blocked by traffic, then *STAY WHERE YOU ARE!* even if you have to wait for the lights to go through another sequence.

Note: on checking whether the road beyond a crossroads or other junction is clear, see also 'Box junctions' on the next page.

TRAFFIC LIGHTS WITH GREEN ARROWS

Green arrow lights (filter lights) can be attached to either side of a set of traffic lights, or be mounted on the lights themselves. When the green arrow lights up, your way should be clear to turn in that direction; sometimes it's before and sometimes it's after the full 'green' phase. (See 'Level crossings', page 68, for more on traffic light signals.)

HINTS & TIPS

In other countries be prepared for different conventions; for example, in the UK they use what is called a 'starting amber' on their traffic lights. This means that the red and amber lights appear together for a number of seconds before the lights turn green.

BOX JUNCTIONS

These were introduced to prevent blockages at crossroads and other junctions.

The rule is:
DO NOT ENTER THE BOX UNLESS YOUR EXIT IS CLEAR.

Usually you will not stop in the yellow box unless, while your exit route is clear, you are caused to wait by oncoming traffic.

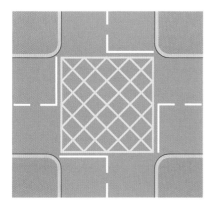

JUNCTIONS

Junctions present some of the worst hazards for drivers.

T-junctions and **staggered junctions** have been shown to be far more dangerous than roundabouts, or even crossroads.

But it's worth noting that a significant number of crashes also occur at **private drives and entrances**.

How to keep crashes at junctions down to a minimum

If you're on a major road where there are junctions with minor roads:
- watch out for vehicles joining from side roads
- don't overtake when you can see there's a junction coming up on either side of the road.

If you're at a junction waiting to join a major road:
- don't proceed until you're sure it's safe. Give way to traffic on the major road.

And remember – **Mirror, Signal, Mirror, Manoeuvre**.

If, when you're waiting to pull out of a side road, an approaching car on the main road indicates left:
- don't pull out until the other vehicle

has actually begun to turn. The driver may suddenly change his or her mind, or the indicator may be flashing in error. Look out for vehicles following the turning car.

What to watch out for at junctions

- cyclists and motorcyclists – take care not to trap a cyclist on the inside when you're turning left.
- pedestrians – they may be crossing a road that you're turning into. *They have priority, so don't hassle them!*

Road markings and signs at junctions

(See also 'Follow the signs', page 69 and 'Crossing the line', page 71.)

If you're joining a major road from a minor road, the signs and road markings will clearly tell you to STOP or YIELD.

HINTS & TIPS

Signposts can be a hazard in themselves if you crash into them at speed. New technology is helping with the growth of more forgiving, deformable and plastic compound poles.

At a STOP sign, you *must* come to a complete stop. YOU WILL FAIL YOUR DRIVING TEST IF YOU DO NOT STOP COMPLETELY AT A STOP SIGN, even if everything else that you do is perfect.

At a YIELD sign, you may not have to stop completely if the road is clear.

Slip roads at junctions

Some major roads – and all motorways – will have slip roads to help you when you're joining.

BUT YOU SHOULD STILL YIELD – rather than shooting ahead to join the major road by overtaking on the left!

See 'Motorway rules', page 92, for information about overtaking on the left when on a motorway.

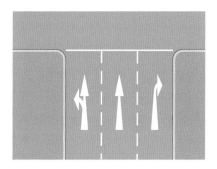

GET IN LANE

A road sign telling you to do this can strike terror into the heart of a novice motorist –

    'Am I in the right lane?'

    'What do I do if I'm not?'

    'Will I have time to move to the lane I need to be in?'

This is yet another occasion when using your *anticipation* skills is vital.

How to deal with lanes

If you're looking well ahead, you should have plenty of time to select the correct lane and to move into it – having first checked that it's safe to do so, by using **Mirror, Signal, Mirror, Manoeuvre** (and again, don't forget the blind spot).

And if you *do* make a mistake – *DON'T PANIC!*

Simply:
- control your speed
- indicate
- transfer to the correct lane in good time, and when there is enough space.

Note: if it's clear that you've left it too late to make the change safely, you should continue in the same lane and find another route to your destination.

Lanes are most frequently found:
- in towns and cities, especially where one-way systems operate
- on dual carriageways and motorways
- on the approaches to roundabouts
- at traffic lights.

HINTS & TIPS

Did you know? There's only one sign which is octagonal: the 'STOP' sign. This is to make it stand out more.

HINTS & TIPS

The only times it's OK to 'overtake' on the left are: when the vehicle in front is signalling to turn right, and there is room for you to pass on the left; in queues on a motorway when a lane to the right is temporarily moving more slowly; and in a one-way street.

LANES AND ROUNDABOUTS

As you come up to a roundabout:

• use progressive braking

This means gentle braking in good time to gradually slow the car. Sudden braking should only ever be necessary in emergencies.

• select the lane you want to be in
• use your indicators to signal if you intend to turn left or right.

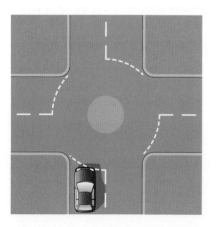

IF YOU'RE TAKING THE EXIT LEADING TO THE ROAD AHEAD –
• don't indicate as you approach, but indicate left as you pass the exit before the one you plan to take.

Remember, on a roundabout the rule is always:
• *give way to traffic from the right.*

Although you're concentrating on positioning your car correctly, you'll find that there are some types of road users who seem to be doing something different.

Vehicles not playing by the rules at roundabouts

Part of your hazard awareness is to know that there are some vehicles that don't keep to the normal lane when approaching a roundabout. This is due to their large size, or vulnerability on the road.

• Cyclists sometimes stay in the left lane while giving an arm signal indicating that they want to turn right. *Slow down* and give them room to move across.
• The same applies to **horse riders.**
• **Long vehicles** may need to begin their right turn by taking up part of the left lane.

Stay well back and give them room to manoeuvre.

Of course – incorrect road positioning may also just be down to bad driving! It is a sad fact of Irish life that we tend to be sloppy about our lane discipline and this is nowhere more evident than at roundabouts. Cars frequently do not signal correctly, and many give the impression that they have never heard of – let alone studied – the *Rules of the Road*. This is another hazard for you to manage.

CHAPTER 2

LANE CLOSURES

These are a frequent feature of **motorways** (see page 95), but are also found on other major roads such as dual carriageways.

They are generally found where there are **road works.**
You'll usually get *plenty of warning* of a lane closure: *traffic signs* will be put up well ahead, and part of the road may be *coned off* before the area of road works.

So – *change lanes in good time.*

It's likely that a *temporary speed limit* will be in operation, so be prepared to drive at a slower speed than is usual for that road.

Sometimes the whole carriageway is closed, with a sign indicating you should cross to the opposite one.

This is called a *contraflow*. Points to remember here are:
• drive even more carefully, as you'll have to keep in very narrow lanes
• stay in the lane you're in.

HINTS & TIPS

In your driving test, where there are lanes the driving tester will check your position on the road; it's important not to be straddling two at a time.

OTHER TYPES OF LANES
Bus lanes
Bus lanes are marked on the road, and usually by signs as well.

Some bus lanes only operate at certain times of the day.

- You're not allowed to drive (or park!) in a bus lane during its hours of operation, or to move into one in order to overtake.

Note: the same rules apply to **tram lanes.**

- In one-way systems, bus lanes sometimes run in the *opposite direction to the rest of the traffic*; this is sometimes true of cycle lanes too.

- If you want to turn left and there is a bus lane or tram lane in operation, *give way* to buses or trams – whichever direction they're coming from.

Cycle tracks
Cycle tracks are marked by signs and by a white line along the road.

If it's a *solid* white line –

it means don't drive or park in it during its times of operation.

If it's a *broken* white line –

you can only drive or park in it if there is no alternative, and not at any time when waiting restrictions apply (see 'Where to park – and where not to', page 78).

PEDESTRIAN CROSSINGS
(See also 'I didn't even see him', page 48.)

There are some general rules that apply to all types of pedestrian crossings.

- *Don't overtake* a vehicle that's slowing down as it approaches a crossing.

- *Don't harass pedestrians* who might be a bit slow, by revving your engine or edging the car forward or any other method.

- As you approach any pedestrian crossing, *slow down and be prepared to stop.*

Zebra crossings

A zebra crossing isn't controlled by pedestrian lights, but usually there's an orange flashing beacon.

The rule here is that you must stop and give way to pedestrians once a person has stepped on to the crossing. Also be prepared for somebody pushing a pram in front of them.

Pelican crossings

These are controlled by lights:
• red for 'STOP' followed by
• flashing amber.

When the amber light is flashing, give way to pedestrians already on the crossing.

Toucan and puffin crossings

These are like pelican crossings, but without the 'flashing' phase.
At toucan crossings, cyclists are allowed to ride across.

HINTS & TIPS

At crossings, where motorists see a red traffic light, pedestrians usually see a green figure (walking), and where motorists see a flashing amber light, pedestrians usually see a flashing green figure.

HINTS & TIPS

In some instances cyclists can use the bus lane, if the sign has symbols for both buses and bicycles.

One crossing or two?

At **zebra** crossings where there's an island in the centre, pedestrians should treat it as two crossings, and wait half-way across the road.

Pelican crossings that go straight across the road count as one crossing even if there's a central island, so you must wait for pedestrians who've started to cross from the other side of the road – *even if the signal for drivers has changed to flashing amber or green by the time they get half-way.*

Staggered crossings

However, if the crossings on either side of the central island are not in a straight line, they count as two *separate crossings* and the pedestrians have to press the button a second time when they're half-way across, and wait for the green light or figure.

CHAPTER 2

LEVEL CROSSINGS

These come in so many different types that two pages in the *Rules of the Road* are devoted to them; you should study these pages carefully.

Most crossings have *warning lights*, *alarm sounds* and *barriers*; but there are some level crossings with no barriers, and crossing these demands great caution. The signs for these are shown below.

Some have gates you operate yourself; there is normally a phone to use before you proceed.

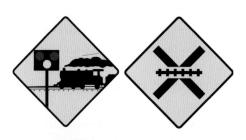

STOP
nuair a lasann na soilse dearga

STOP When Red Lights Show

HINTS & TIPS

You may also come across brown signs, which show places of interest to tourists, and orange signs which are used at the location of road works.

At crossings with automatic barriers:
- Don't try to speed up to get across as the barrier comes down, or attempt to zigzag around half-barriers.
- If the barrier stays down after the train's gone, it means there's another train coming.

What if your car breaks down half-way across?
- get all the passengers out and tell them to move away from the crossing
- if there's a railway phone, use it to alert the signal operator
- attempt to move your vehicle, *but only if there's time before the train comes*
- if necessary, call 999 (or 112) and inform the Gardai.

HINTS & TIPS

Although the Rules of the Road shows modern versions of the signs, you may find more old-fashioned signs still in use in some places.

FOLLOW THE SIGNS

The roadsides of Ireland are festooned with signs. There are so many that at times it seems as if drivers will suffer from information overload. Apart from the whole host of commercial messages that bombard us, there are three main types of road signs. These are:

- regulatory signs
- warning signs
- information signs

Regulatory signs

Much of what you can and can't do as a driver is governed by Regulatory Signs. These indicate what you have to do under road traffic law, and you must obey them. They are divided into three groups:

upright signs
road markings
traffic lights

Upright signs generally come in two formats: a white background with a red border and a black lettering, or a blue background with a white symbol or letter. They can be round, triangular or octagonal (the distinctive 'Stop' sign). You are likely to be very familiar with them having seen them all your life, but you need to be clear on their specific meanings for the Driving Test.

Warning signs

These signs warn you of a hazard ahead, like a dangerous bend or a junction, a roundabout or anything that would make you need to drive more carefully. You must always take heed of these warning signs, which are always in the same format.

They are diamond shaped, have a yellow background with a black border, and use a black symbol to show what the hazard is.

Information signs

As the name implies, these are signs that give information about your location, directions and distance.

Information signs are in different colours depending on their location. On motorways they are blue with white lettering, on national roads they are green with white lettering, and on regional and local roads they are white with black lettering. There are also temporary directional signs which are put up by the AA. These are yellow with black lettering.

You'll find a set of the more commonly used road signs printed in your copy of the *Rules of the Road*.

HINTS & TIPS

Motorway signs are blue; signs on national primary roads are green. Distances marked are in kilometres to the centre of the town or city indicated.

ROAD SIGNS AND YOUR DRIVING TEST

As part of your test, the driving tester will show you a photograph of a number of road traffic signs and you are expected to know what they mean. When you take your test, you should be able to demonstrate by your driving that you know and understand all the signs and road markings along the route.

You'll be expected to look ahead and be *aware* of them in advance (see 'Anticipation', page 48) so that you can react to them in good time.

When you take your **Theory Test,** you're likely to find questions on one or more of these:
- the different sign shapes
- the meanings of individual signs
- what sorts of signs to expect at certain road systems (such as a one-way street, or a contraflow)
- how you should react when you see a particular sign.

But however differently the questions are worded – it all comes down to how well you know the *Rules of the Road*.

CROSSING THE LINE

A guide to white lines and other road markings.

White lines can be found on the road going at different angles:

- across the road (telling you to stop, give way etc.)
- along the road (indicating the centre, or dividing the road into lanes etc.).

Lines across the road

(These are used in conjunction with road signs, see page 69.) As a general rule, more paint on the road signals more danger.

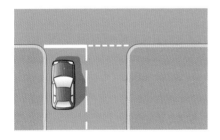

A **single continuous** white line across the road in front of you means STOP.

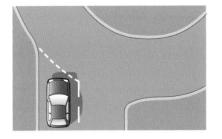

HINTS & TIPS

When you come to a junction the driving tester may ask you to make a turn; but you're expected to watch out for lane markings on the road and signs giving directions, and to make decisions about how to react to these yourself.

A **single broken** white line is used at roundabouts to indicate 'give way to traffic from the right'. It is also found at the end of the slip roads to dual carriageways and motorways.

Lines along the road

The centre line of most roads is marked with a white line. This may be a single line or a double line and it may be continuous or broken. You must keep to the left of this line.

You cannot cross a continuous line (unless it is for access or in an emergency). You cannot cross a broken white line unless it is safe to do so. If there is a double white line it is usually because there are different instructions depending on which side of the road that you are on. *You must obey the line closest to you.*

The edge of the road may be marked with a continuous or a broken yellow line. These lines also indicate hard shoulders on non-motorway roads. You may not drive in the hard shoulder, but you are allowed use it in certain circumstances. For example, you may move to the left to facilitate an overtaking manoeuvre by the car behind. Other yellow lines along the edge – single or double – are related to parking.

So here are the rules again in detail:

Broken white lines

A **broken white** line is used to mark the centre of the road.
ONLY CROSS IT
when

• you can see that the road is clear, so you move out to overtake a slow vehicle

or

• when you turn right off the road.

In the diagram, left, hatched markings in the middle of the main road allow you a waiting space when turning right, in addition to the broken white lines.

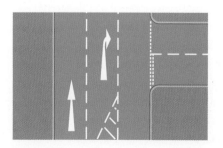

Double white lines where the one nearest to you is a broken line and the other a solid line

This means you can cross the line, for example to overtake – as long as you can see far enough ahead to complete the manoeuvre before another solid white line starts on your side.

Double white lines

The general rule is don't cross where the lines are double – it won't be safe to do so.
When can you cross the lines?

• in an emergency
• if turning right
• if you have to pass a stationary vehicle
• if you have to overtake a horse and rider, a slow-moving road maintenance vehicle, or a cyclist.

HINTS & TIPS

Look out for curved white arrows on the road – these are put there to remind you to get back on your side!

SPEED LIMITS

The rule is:

*KEEP TO THE SPEED LIMIT
SHOWN FOR –*

• the road you're on

and

• the vehicle you're driving.

It's safe to assume the limit will be 50kph in a built-up area, which is where you are likely to be driving during your Driving Test, although there may also be 60kph zones. The Irish Driving Test does not include any higher speed driving, although your driving lessons certainly should.

It is interesting to note that the safest roads that we have, statistically, are the motorways; yet learners are not permitted to use them. Although they are high speed they don't have any junctions, they have good surfaces and the carriageways are separated. Hence they can carry a 120kph speed limit.

There are also what are termed HGDCs – High Grade Dual Carriageways. These do not quite meet the criteria for motorway status – there may be occasional entrance roads for example – but they are close to motorway standard and some have been given the 120kph speed limit. This is as fast as any driver should ever go, unless you are on a test track.

The speed limits shown in the table below are maximum speeds. Weather conditions, night driving, driving behind cyclists or motorcyclists, and adjusting for bends in the road will all have an effect on your speed – so you'll very often be below the limit where speed is concerned. In fact many drivers seem to think that it is wrong to travel below the speed limit. This is not true.

CHAPTER 2

Type of road:	Speed Limit
Motorway	120kph
National Road (Primary and Secondary)	100kph
Non-national road (Regional & Local)	80kph
Urban and suburban (and elsewhere where applicable)	60kph
Built-up areas	50kph
Pedestrian areas (where applied by the local authority)	30kph

There are other types of speed limits. For example, there are special speed limits that apply to trucks and buses, or that apply while towing. These are all explained in detail in the *Rules of the Road*.

The important thing is to obey them. To state the obvious, you may not break the speed limit during your Driving Test. More importantly, they have been applied for good reason. If a low speed limit doesn't make sense to you, remember that an engineer has assessed the road and recommended it, and in any case no one is allowed to decide which laws they obey and which they don't. Speeding is one of our major killers, and Gardai are focusing on it.

If you do break the speed limit you face a fine and having two penalty points applied to your licence (or four if you dispute the case and lose in court).

STOPPING DISTANCES

It's worth spending a bit of time getting your head round this. You are likely to be asked questions about stopping distances in your Theory Test, and in any case it's important to understand and allow for braking distances, which are often longer than you think.

What are stopping distances tables meant to do?

Although you have to 'learn' them to pass your Theory Test, it's important to understand their purpose. You'll build up experience while driving of how much space you need to leave between you and the car in front so that, if need be, you could stop suddenly if that vehicle did the same. However, so that you don't build up that experience by means of a series of 'near-misses', the 'stopping distances' chart opposite is a good guide.

Speed	Thinking distance	Braking distance	Overall stopping distance
30kph	5.5 metres	5.3 metres	10.8 metres or 3 car lengths
50kph	9.2 metres	14.8 metres	24 metres or 6 car lengths
60kph	11 metres	21.4 metres	32.4 metres or 9 car lengths
80kph	14.7 metres	38 metres	52.7 metres or 13 car lengths
100kph	18.3 metres	59.4 metres	77.7 metres or 18 car lengths
120kph	22 metres	85.5 metres	107.5 metres or 24 car lengths

Note: an average car length is 4 metres (13 feet).

Remember:
YOUR STOPPING DISTANCE IS MADE UP OF YOUR THINKING DISTANCE + YOUR BRAKING DISTANCE.

overall stopping distance 24m

50kph → **thinking 9.2m** | **braking 14.8m** |

CHAPTER 2

> ### HINTS & TIPS
> Don't forget that motorcycles and large vehicles may have longer stopping distances than cars.

> ### HINTS & TIPS
> HGVs are limited to a maximum speed of 80kph, and they are also not permitted to use the right-hand lane of a motorway.

If you are faced with a sudden hazard on the road it takes a moment for your brain to process the information and decide to brake and for your right foot to reach the pedal. This is the 'thinking time' or 'reaction time', during which the car continues its forward motion. Once you have applied the brakes it takes a period of time for your car to slow to a stop – the braking distance. There are many variables in each of these times: the speed of your reactions may be different depending on how alert you are feeling, how well you are concentrating, and even how recently you have eaten.

Braking distance will also vary. It will depend on the quality of your brakes and tyres and also on road conditions.

It's not unknown for Theory Test candidates to protest that they were marked wrong on a question that they thought they had got right – because they weren't clear about the differences between Thinking Distance, Braking Distance and Overall Stopping Distance.

For test purposes, you simply have to learn them. Once your test is behind you and you are out on the road, you need to understand them and understand how they vary. Be prudent and allow extra distance. A near miss, even if your reactions were brilliant, proves that you were too close in the first place.

> ### HINTS & TIPS
> The power to set speed limits rests not with the Gardai or the government, but with the individual local authorities. This can cause some problems, and the AA has complained about the lack of consistency from one area to another.

TEST YOUR UNDERSTANDING OF THIS SECTION

1. When two vehicles are approaching an unmarked crossroads, which one has priority?
2. For what reason could you decide to wait in a box junction before your exit is clear?
3. You're turning left on to a main road from a side road, and you can see a car approaching from the right and indicating left. How can you be sure that the road is clear for you to proceed?
4. What shape of road marking means 'Yield'?
5. What action should you take if you realise you're in the wrong lane?
6. What is the key rule to remember at roundabouts?
7. At what times, if any, are you allowed to drive in a cycle lane marked by a solid white line?
8. Do you have to stop at a zebra crossing if a pedestrian has not actually put their foot on it?
9. What are the three main types of traffic sign?
10. What is meant by a solid white line in the centre of the road?
11. If you're driving in a road where there are street lights, what is the usual speed limit?
12. Is there any difference in the speed limits for motorways and National Primary Roads?
13. What factors may affect your reaction time when you decide to brake?
14. Is it good driving practice to drive at the maximum speed allowed by the speed limit for the road you're on?
15. What is meant by progressive braking?

ANSWERS ON PAGES 166–7

CHAPTER 2

YOU CAN'T PARK THERE!

Parking is a subject which causes a great deal of aggravation, to drivers, pedestrians and home-owners alike; and as more and more cars appear on our roads, the problems associated with parking just seem to get worse.

The question to keep in mind is –
• will I be breaking the law, or causing inconvenience or danger to anyone, if I decide to park in a particular place?

As the title of this section implies, it's easier to list the places where you *can't* park than those where you *can!*

You'll find a summary of forbidden parking places on pages 79–80. But first, assuming you succeed in finding a parking place on the road, here are a few points to remember.
• Park as close as you can to the kerb, and parallel to it.
• Park in the direction of traffic flow if you can.
• Don't leave the car with its wheels half-on and half-off the kerb – this is illegal.
• Leave just enough space for your car and others to get in and out comfortably. Take care not to block others in, and don't take up more than one space.
• Before you leave the car, check that you've put the handbrake on and have left the car in a low gear (usually first or reverse). For automatics, engage 'P'.
• Be careful opening the door! There could be a car or a cyclist coming.
• Passengers should get out on the kerb side.
• Lock the vehicle when you leave it.
• Fold in your wing mirrors (if they have that facility).

WHERE TO PARK – AND WHERE NOT TO

When driving in town it's sensible to use:
• purpose-built car parks
• parking meter zones
• park-and-ride schemes.

HINTS & TIPS

Remember – take your time when reversing, and don't be hurried by what you imagine other drivers might be thinking about you!

Finding parking places out of town is generally easier, but you may still encounter restrictions (such as residents' parking schemes) – and some country lanes are just too narrow to park in safely.

When you *know* that parking is likely to be a problem, it's better to use public transport, or to walk or cycle instead (while gaining environmental 'brownie points' at the same time!).

Deciding where to park

Always look for **traffic signs** or **road markings** indicating that you shouldn't park. Here are some of the common 'no-go' areas for parking:

- any part of a motorway – this includes the hard shoulder, and motorway approach roads (slip roads). When on a motorway, the service areas are the only safe places to park.
- any road which is a 'clearway' during the times shown
- bus, cycle or tram lanes during their hours of operation (see page 66)
- pedestrian crossings and the approaches to them; it is an offence to park within 15 metres before or five metres after any pedestrian crossing.
- approaches to level crossings (see page 68)

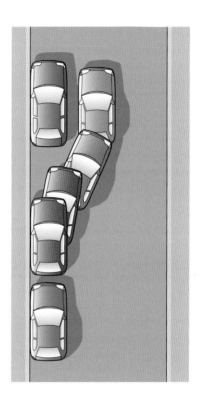

In addition to these places, road signs and road markings will tell you whether parking is legal or not. There are locations where parking is legal only within certain times. In urban areas there are clearways where you are not even allowed to stop during the periods indicated. Yellow lines may allow you to load or unload goods or passengers at certain times.

Get to know these different road markings, and look out for them when you're out driving or on foot. You have to obey parking rules. Many people

HINTS & TIPS

Bad parking is a major cause of traffic congestion in Irish towns and cities. Life would be a lot easier for us all if we all played by the rules.

think it's a trivial issue to ignore them but it's not; it is a major inconvenience for businesses and for other drivers, and if you park badly enough to block sightlines for other traffic or pedestrians it can be dangerous.

You should also note that a lot of towns and cities now use clamping to deter illegal parking. You'll find a more comprehensive explanation of all of this in the *Rules of the Road*.

Other places not to park

- at a bus stop
- at the entrance to a school
- across a driveway
- in a space reserved for disabled people
- obstructing entrances and exits used by emergency services
- opposite a continuous white line when your car would force traffic to cross that line in order to pass by
- close to a junction
- on the brow of a hill
- on a bend.

Four cars in the diagram below are parked illegally or inconsiderately – can you spot which ones?

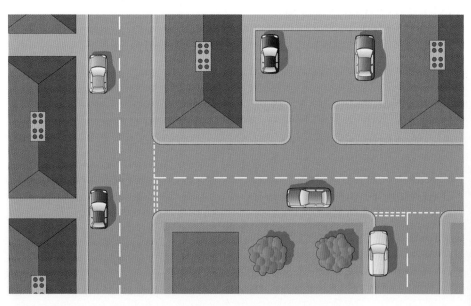

HINTS & TIPS

You may have seen a driver park and rush into a house or shop having switched on their hazard warning lights. This has no legal status whatsoever, and it doesn't give anyone an exemption from parking rules!

PARKING AT NIGHT

You need to be more careful when parking at night, and even more conscious of the need not to block the view of other drivers or pedestrians. Choose a well lit spot if you can, and you may also need to leave on your sidelights or parking lights.

PARKING AND YOUR DRIVING TEST

You have to carry out a parking manoeuvre as part of your Driving Test, although you do not yet have to perform a 'parallel parking' manoeuvre. It is a good idea to practice parking for other reasons. It helps you learn the skills of reversing and observation – which you also need for the test – and of course it is something that drivers have to do every day. You should be able to carry out the manoeuvre swiftly and smoothly with minimum inconvenience to others around you.

TEST YOUR UNDERSTANDING OF THIS SECTION

1. How should you position your car when parking in the street?
2. Where should you look for places to park in town centres?
3. Can you park in a 'Disabled' space in a car park if you are quite sure all the other spaces are full?
4. Why do you need to be careful opening your door?
5. How can bad parking be dangerous to others?

Answers on page 167

HINTS & TIPS

If you are parking beside a disabled space, or whenever you are parking beside a car which displays a disabled person's parking permit, try to leave a little extra space; they may need more room to manoeuvre.

DRIVING UNDER THE INFLUENCE

Where alcohol and drugs are concerned, there's a short answer to all questions about whether to drive while under the influence – *DON'T!*

ALCOHOL

Young people are better informed and overall seem to have a more 'mature' attitude than their elders about the dangers of drinking and driving. There have been many public education and advertising campaigns about this in recent times. Sadly, given the sheer scale of the problem over the years, many people of all ages have had personal experience of being in a road accident, or know of a friend or relative who has been killed or hurt.

In many cases groups of young people make a very sensible decision when they're going out: the nominated driver doesn't drink alcohol during the evening. But young people are not immune to the temptation to drink and drive, and there are those who will take risks with drink or other drugs. In fact car crash statistics show that for alcohol, as for other causes of crashes, males between the ages of 19 and 34 have the highest risk.

Even at levels well below the legal limit the risk of having a car crash increases very sharply. Ireland's limit of 80 milligrams of alcohol per 100 millilitres of blood is the highest in Europe, and there are good arguments for reducing it. In the meantime, especially for inexperienced drivers, common sense says do not mix any alcohol with driving.

Alcohol, even at low levels, reduces reaction time and impairs judgement. It also magnifies risk-taking and aggressive behaviour as well as inducing feelings of euphoria. It preferentially affects the human eye's ability to see light at the red end of the

HINTS & TIPS

In 2006 a team led by Dr Declan Bedford studied the data from all road crashes that occurred in Ireland in 2003. Among other things, they found that alcohol was a factor in 37% of all fatal crashes. Pedestrian alcohol was a factor in 38% of pedestrian fatalities. It also seems to be more of a male than a female problem: in almost 90% of crashes where driver alcohol was a causal factor, the driver was male.

spectrum, which means that night vision is less acute. This is not a combination that you want when you are moving a ton of steel at high speed.

The Road Safety Authority recently released the results of a study *(by Dr Declan Bedford et al, 2006)* that showed that alcohol was a contributory cause in as many as 36.5% of all fatal crashes in Ireland. It is also a factor in 62% of all single-vehicle crashes. If you are curious about the research which the experts find so conclusive you can have a look yourself. A quick internet search will bring up a huge amount of information.

The RSA website is excellent, and you can also find very good information at www.aaireland.ie. But for further detail on the effects of alcohol and other substances on driving, there is the International Council on Alcohol, Drugs and Traffic Safety; which is at www.icadts.org

These are alarming statistics. It seems unbelievable that we can allow so many of our citizens to die because there are drivers who take such insane risks. However, we are getting better at enforcing the law. The Garda now have much greater powers to breathalyse drivers, and are currently carrying out 30,000 breath tests per month. For the chronic drink driver, it is no longer a question of if he or she gets caught, but when.

The legal limit for alcohol when driving is described as follows:

- 35 microgrammes of alcohol in 100 millilitres of breath

or
- 80 milligrams of alcohol in 100 millilitres of blood

or
- 107 milligrams of alcohol in 100 millilitres of urine.

CHAPTER 2

HINTS & TIPS

Drugs and driving is a growing problem. Research by the Department of Forensic Medicine at UCD examined 2,000 driver blood samples as part of a study in 2000 and 2001. The samples were taken from drivers whom the Gardai had stopped because they believed that they were under the influence. The Medical Bureau looked at 1,000 cases that were positive for alcohol and 1,000 that were negative. They found traces of some drug among 15.7% of the sample, with cannabis being the most common. More recent research has produced similar findings.

How many pints is that?

No one can say without guessing. You cannot know how many pints of beer or glasses of wine make up the legal limit, because the effects of the same size of drink can vary considerably from person to person. You may be affected much more quickly if you drink alcohol on an empty stomach, or if you're not well. Females will show a higher level than males after consuming the same amount, and the rate of absorption varies based on a number of factors. Some things are constant, however:

- It's not possible to bring down your alcohol level by drinking coffee.
- If you have a drink at lunchtime, you probably still won't be safe to drive by the evening.
- The same applies to drinking in the evening and driving the following morning.

The **penalties** for driving under the influence of alcohol are listed in full in the *Rules of the Road*, and as you would expect they are fairly hefty, including mandatory **disqualification** and heavy fines. The **cost of insuring your car** will also go up if you have a drink-driving conviction.

Be warned also about driving the following morning. If you feel hung over, it is virtually certain that there is still too much alcohol in your system for you to drive. The Gardai are conducting breath testing in the mornings as well as the evenings.

DRUGS

All of the risks associated with driving after drinking alcohol are, of course, equally associated with driving under the influence of other drugs. There are various narcotics in widespread use in Ireland. Perhaps the most noticeable of these are cannabis, cocaine and its derivatives, ecstasy, and opiates (heroin). While these do differ, all share the following characteristics:

- You may become unreasonably confident about your skill as a driver, and take more risks.
- Your co-ordination will be affected and your reactions will be slower than normal.
- Your hazard awareness will be diminished.
- You will be less accurate when

judging distance, and the speed of other vehicles.

It's more difficult to assess the effects of drugs than the effects of alcohol – *they may well be stronger.*

Irish law has an offence of 'impaired driving'. It operates in the same way as the law on drink driving and has similar punishments. So it doesn't matter what substance does the impairing, you have to be sober in order to drive.

But –
WHAT ABOUT DRUGS PRESCRIBED BY YOUR DOCTOR?

This is a very important issue, and you should be very careful when driving if you are taking any medication.

- Pay attention to information or warnings about driving given on the label (see 'Alertness', page 54).
- Check with your doctor or pharmacist about whether the medicine prescribed will affect your ability to drive safely.
- A common side effect of some medicines (e.g. cough medicines) is to make you feel drowsy. Tiredness is one of the most frequent causes of accidents (see 'Alertness', page 54) – and it's one of the reasons to take extra care when **driving at night**.

TEST YOUR UNDERSTANDING OF THIS SECTION

1. How many breath tests are the Gardai conducting each month?
2. When going out for an evening with friends, what can you do to avoid being caught for drink-driving?
3. If you drink alcohol in the evening, is there any reason why you should not drive the following morning?
4. What are the main effects of drugs and alcohol on your driving ability?
5. How does the law deal with drug driving as opposed to drink driving?

ANSWERS ON PAGE 167

CHAPTER 2

HINTS & TIPS

A recent study by the International Council on Alcohol, Drugs and Traffic Safety (www.icadts.org) looked at a sample of 2,871 crashes that occurred in California and Florida. The study showed that a statistically significant increase in accident risk began at the 40 milligram level – half the current Irish legal maximum. Risk increased dramatically with higher concentrations that were still below our legal maximum.

IT'S DIFFERENT AT NIGHT

If you learn to drive in the winter, you may have some lessons in the dark; but if not, you can take and pass your test without having much idea about how to adjust your driving technique for **driving at night.**

On the one hand:
- headlights can give you more warning of oncoming traffic than you would get in the day

but on the other hand:
- hazards are more difficult to see in the dark
- pedestrians may behave more erratically – for example, at closing time for pubs – and they may not *all* be wearing light-coloured clothing as recommended, still less reflective armbands!
- if you haven't kept your screen wash filled up and replaced faulty wipers (see 'Look after your car...', pages 35–6), your windscreen will become almost impossible to see through in the dark because of grease smears etc.
- your field of vision is generally narrower than in daylight
- you run the risk of being dazzled by the headlights of an oncoming car if they are badly adjusted, or

deliberately too bright (see page 99 in Chapter 3).

You'll need to make allowances for the increased risks. So:
- Check that your **lights** are all working properly.
- Drive more slowly than the maximum speed limit.
- Watch out for cyclists and pedestrians.

LIGHTING UP THE NIGHT
Sidelights
Your sidelights (and the lights on the rear registration plate) should always be on at night.

Headlights
Headlights are also necessary on most roads. Your copy of the *Rules of the Road* tells you to turn on your lights at dusk, but in practice you should have **dipped headlights** on almost constantly. In fact in some countries this is a legal requirement.

HINTS & TIPS

Use dipped headlights in the day as well, whenever it's gloomy and/or raining.

HINTS & TIPS

In the depths of an Irish winter, darkness lasts for 16 hours per day. Even during daylight visibility is often poor.

Full beam headlights are only used for country driving, where there are no street lights, and should be turned off whenever another vehicle comes into view ahead of you or is approaching on the opposite carriageway. (See 'I'm right behind you!', page 103.)

Fog lights

In normal night-time conditions there's no need to switch these on; only use them in poor visibility (100 metres or less), and switch them off again as soon as visibility improves. The unnecessary use of over-bright fog lights is an increasing symptom of driver aggression (see 'I'm right behind you!', as above).

FRONT FOG LIGHTS ARE NOT A FASHION STATEMENT!

Turn back to 'Look after your car', pages 31–2, and remind yourself of the **legal requirements** for headlights and fog lights. The alignment of your headlights will be checked as part of your car's NCT test.

TEST YOUR UNDERSTANDING OF THIS SECTION

1. Why should you take even more care when driving at night?
2. When should you use dipped headlights?
3. Is it correct to use full beam headlights when driving on a motorway?
4. When are fog lights necessary?
5. What is the effect of night driving on your field of vision?

ANSWERS ON PAGES 168

HINTS & TIPS

Did you know that it's illegal to drive with faulty lights? Carry spares and fuses – in some countries this is a legal requirement.

STORMY WEATHER

Just as for night driving, you need to adjust your driving technique for different weather conditions.

If there's been a sudden downpour there may be water covering the road surface, making it difficult to control the car; and excessive speed may result in 'aquaplaning': rather like skidding, but on water, because the tyres cannot grip effectively.

In order not to slide gracefully into the car in front –

KEEP YOUR DISTANCE!

HINTS & TIPS

Remember that in older cars, having lots of the electrical features switched on at the same time (such as lights, rear window heater) can cause the car to stall when you start the engine. When you re-start the engine, switch off all non-essential equipment. Once the engine is running, let it warm up before you switch the extras back on.

DRIVING ON ICY ROADS

Ice on the road is one of the most treacherous conditions you'll encounter; the best advice is not to drive unless it's really necessary, but if you *must* make the journey –

- Allow plenty of room between you and other vehicles; your stopping distance in these conditions can be *ten times* more than usual.
- Drive slowly; but *in as high a gear as possible* (to make your progress smoother).
- Accelerate carefully.
- Use progressive braking.
- Be very careful when steering round bends.

Conditions can change suddenly from one stretch of road to the next, and you may hit a patch of **black ice** without warning. One clue that this has happened is that your wheels will make almost no sound.

However careful you try to be, you may have to cope with a **skid** at some stage when driving in icy conditions (see page 104).

HINTS & TIPS

Remember the two second rule (see 'Motorists with attitude', on page 46)? Well, you can 'Say it again, when driving in rain'! In other words, you need to allow at least twice the distance for braking and stopping in wet weather.

DRIVING IN SNOW

Once again, the best advice is DON'T unless you really have to.

If you must, then get yourself kitted out with emergency supplies and rescue gear. These can be carried in the boot all through winter. Include items like:

• a spade
• blankets or extra coats
• practical footwear (in case you have to walk some distance).

Also consider carrying some food and hot drinks.

All this might sound a bit over the top, but you won't enjoy the experience if you break down in freezing weather and have to wait for help to arrive…

In some countries, special snow tyres and snow chains (that fit around the tyres) are compulsory in winter. We are a little luckier in Ireland, and very seldom have to deal with a serious fall of snow.

Before you start

Clear ice and snow from windows, mirrors and number plate before you get moving, and make sure the lights aren't obscured by ice or grime.

Don't start driving until your front and rear screens are fully demisted.

It's illegal to start driving while your car has any snow left on it; this is because when the car warms up, the snow can block your field of vision, or dazzle you, as it slides off.

On the road

It's quite possible for road markings to get covered up by snow; and you may not be too sure where the edge of the road is. If in doubt – YIELD! (This also applies when driving in fog – see page 90.)

Note: In snow, motorcyclists may take advantage of the tracks formed by cars and drive along them; this may cause them to take up a different position on the road from normal.

CHAPTER 2

ON THE SKIDS

The technique for dealing with skids can take a bit of learning at first. Bear in mind that this is not something that you practise on the road. If you get the opportunity to learn in a test track environment then fine, but remember that no matter how expert you become, the best drivers are the ones who are careful enough to avoid the situation in the first place. In foul winter weather, the best driving decision is often to stay at home.

For a **rear-wheel skid:**
Unless your car has ABS (see below), take your foot off the brake so that the wheels are free to turn, and re-apply immediately. At the same time, if the skid is not in a straight line, *steer in the same direction as the skid* to regain control.

Anti-Lock Braking System (ABS)

Because skidding occurs when the wheels lose their grip on the road surface, ABS gives no advantage once the car has gone into a skid. However, ABS will allow you to steer the car on slippery surfaces, because it applies and releases the brakes to maximum effect without locking the wheels; all you have to do is keep your foot firmly on the brake pedal.

DRIVING IN FOG

Driving in fog is always hazardous. Some techniques are more effective than others.

- *Slow down* as you drive into the fog – but remember to check your mirror first.
- Don't stick too closely behind the vehicle in front. You need to have room to stop safely if necessary. *Remember:* double the two second rule.
- Use **dipped headlights and rear foglights** if visibility is down to

HINTS & TIPS

The main cause of skids is the driver, who either brakes too hard, accelerates fiercely or steers harshly.

100m or less, and use **front fog lights,** if you have them – and if they give the best visibility.
• Keep your screen clear with the wipers and demisters.
If you have to negotiate a junction in dense fog, this is one of the times when it's a good idea to use your horn (see 'Sound that horn', page 105).

Once the fog has cleared, remember to switch the fog lights off, as they will dazzle other drivers when conditions are normal (see page 104).

For advice on motorway driving in fog, see the next section.

TEST YOUR UNDERSTANDING OF THIS SECTION

1. How should you adjust your braking and stopping distances for wet or icy conditions?
2. How should you deal with skidding on an icy road?
3. What precautions do you need to take when driving in snow?
4. In fog, is it best to stay close to the vehicle in front so that you can follow their rear lights?
5. What should you always do when you see that the fog has cleared?

ANSWERS ON PAGE 168

MOTORWAY RULES

Motorways are unique in that different traffic laws apply to them. They are constructed to be safe for fast moving traffic, and very slow vehicles (under 50kph) are not allowed to use them. They are safe because there are no traffic lights, roundabouts or junctions. There is always a hard shoulder for emergencies and the opposite carriageways are separated, either by a wide median or by a physical barrier, or both. This is why they can carry the high speed limit of 120kph.

You never stop or turn on a motorway. You always enter or leave it by means of slip road (sometimes called 'on and off ramps' or 'entry and exit ramps'). You use the slip road either to build up to or slow down from motorway speeds, so that on the main carriageway all vehicles can cruise without needing to adjust their speed.

As with other roads, the rule is that you keep left. The left hand lane is by convention called the 'inside' lane. The 'outside' lane is for overtaking, or you may use it when approaching an on-ramp to allow traffic to join the

motorway - but you should never cruise in it. On a three lane motorway (or multi-lane, but those are very rare in Ireland) the same 'keep left' rule applies.

Learner drivers aren't allowed on motorways, so you can't get experience of what it's like to drive on them until you've passed your test – although as mentioned before, some dual carriageways now come fairly close to motorway conditions.

However, you do need to know all about motorway rules before taking your test, and your Theory Test may also include a question about motorways.

HINTS & TIPS

Motorways are statistically the safest roads that we have. According to a 2005 report published by the AA under the European Road Assessment Programme, Irish motorways have a risk rate of 2.3 fatalities per billion vehicle kilometres. The risk rate on a single carriageway road is ten times higher.

Motorways are a little bit daunting at first but remember that they are the safest roads that we have once you obey the rules. Just remember to enter and exit carefully and to stay alert and mind your lane discipline when you are on the road. Know which exit you want to take in advance. NEVER attempt to reverse back along the hard shoulder towards an exit that you have missed – this is extremely dangerous. Drive on to the next exit and turn back there.

If you learn to drive with a reputable driving school you may be offered the chance of a lesson in motorway driving with your instructor. It makes sense to take up this opportunity.

MOTORWAY DO'S AND DON'TS

DO –

- Carry out **all regular checks** on your vehicle before starting a long motorway journey (see 'Safety first', page 14).
- Join the motorway by building up your speed while on the slip road to match the flow of traffic in the left-hand lane, then use **MSMM**.
- *Give way* to traffic already on the motorway when joining from a slip road.
- Make use of your mirrors frequently,

HINTS & TIPS

The outside lane of a motorway can't be used by: vehicles pulling trailers, goods vehicles weighing over 7.5 tonnes, and passenger vehicles over 7.5 tonnes or over 12 metres in length, or adapted to carry more than 8 passengers plus the driver.

and look well ahead, before you move to another lane to overtake or to leave the motorway. *Check over your shoulder* for blind spots.
- *Take breaks* to avoid tiredness or falling asleep at the wheel.
- Observe **special signs** ordering lower speed limits due to bad weather or road-works (see 'Traffic signs', page 95).
- Keep to the **left** lane except when overtaking, and *return to it* once it's safe to do so.

Be aware that although the general rule is to stay in the **left-hand lane**, there are times when you need to stay in the centre or right-hand lane for a while; eg when a line of slow-moving vehicles are moving along the left lane on an upward gradient. Stay in the centre or right hand lane until you have passed the hazard, then signal if necessary and return to the left.

CHAPTER 2

ON THE ROAD

HINTS & TIPS

Motorways allow for safe long distance cruising, but this very aspect of safety has its own danger: fatigue. Drivers are more prone to fatigue and to the losses of concentration that it causes when on long motorway journeys. Remember to take regular breaks, and to share the driving with someone else if you can.

DON'T –
- *REVERSE –*
  PARK –
  WALK –
  or *drive the wrong way* along the motorway!
- Exceed the **speed limit** (check the table on page 73).
- *Accelerate to a dangerous speed* when joining from a slip road.
- Allow yourself to be influenced by surrounding motorists to *drive faster than you intend*. Drive at a speed where you know you are in control (as long as it's not so slow that you become a hazard to other drivers).
- *Overtake on the left.* The only time when you can appear to 'overtake' on the left is when traffic is moving **slowly** in all lanes, and the left lane is moving faster than the one to the right for a while.

- *Weave in and out* of the lanes of traffic.
- *Cut in sharply* after you overtake.
- Get out and pick up anything that falls from your car on to the road – *stop at the next emergency phone* or stop and use your mobile to tell the Gardai what has happened.

Posts on the edge of the motorway (see below) show the way to the nearest emergency phone.

For all other information relating to motorway driving, see your copy of the *Rules of the Road*.

TRAFFIC SIGNS AND ROAD MARKINGS ON MOTORWAYS
Light signals

On some motorways you may find signs above the roadway, or on the central reservation, that are activated as needed, to warn of accidents, lane closures or weather conditions.

These overhead gantries display arrows or red crosses showing which lanes are open or closed to traffic, and which lanes to move to when motorways merge or diverge. They may also show temporary speed limits.

HINTS & TIPS

Junctions and exits are signposted well in advance so that you can be sure to be in the exit lane in time. There are then 'countdown markers' at 100 metre intervals before the exit slip-road begins.

Direction signs

Direction signs on motorways are blue with white lettering; this distinguishes them from those on other major roads, which are green. Once you see blue signs, you know that you are on a motorway and that the motorway rules apply.

USING THE HARD SHOULDER IN AN EMERGENCY

If you can tell there's a problem developing with your vehicle while on the motorway, turn off at the next exit.

If that's not possible, you'll have to stop your car on the hard shoulder.
* Stop as far to the left as possible, and if you can, near an emergency phone. Switch on your hazard warning lights.

Note: While there are emergency phones at regular intervals along the motorway, these days they are seldom used. Most drivers have a mobile phone available and use that. This is

CHAPTER 2

HINTS & TIPS

Never underestimate how dangerous the hard shoulder can be. As many as one in eight road deaths happen there.

fine, but remember that you will have to know your location. Take note of the road number and junction number, and try to have a fair idea of your location as you go along. If you do find yourself stuck, note that the emergency phones are numbered. Tell the operator which number is on the phone nearest to you and that may help them to pin down exactly where you are.

- Use the *left-hand door* to get out of the vehicle; make sure your passengers do too.
- Keep everyone a*way from the carriageway* – up on the bank if possible.
- Animals should stay in the vehicle, unless you are sure they would not be safe there.
- When you make your call for help give full details of your vehicle and location to the Gardai; tell them if you feel especially at risk for any reason. Then go back and wait in a safe place near the vehicle.

TEST YOUR UNDERSTANDING OF THIS SECTION

1. How can learner drivers get experience of motorway driving?
2. What should you always do before starting out on a long motorway journey?
3. What is the procedure for joining a motorway from a slip road?
4. What is the usual speed limit on a motorway?
5. In what circumstances could you 'overtake on the left' on a motorway?
6. Vehicles slower than what speed are forbidden to use motorways?
7. What type of road sign tells you that you are on a motorway?
8. In what circumstances do you use the outside lane?
9. What types of vehicles are prevented from using the outside lane?
10. For what reason are you allowed to stop on the hard shoulder?

ANSWERS ON PAGES 168–9

CHAPTER 2

OTHER ROAD USERS

HOW'S MY EVOLUTION – MAN, KIND, OR STILL AN APE?

A car is not an offensive weapon; but sadly, it has the potential to become one. A car is not a piece of private territory to be defended. It is first and foremost a method of transport.

When you go out driving, do you feel:
- as if you're going onto a sports field – in competition with other drivers and on your guard against them?

or

- as if you're in solidarity with others, looking to cooperate and thinking only in terms of getting safely to your destination?

You often see professional truck drivers acting cooperatively; i.e. letting each other out of side roads, warning each other of danger. Our roads are becoming more crowded all the time; driving in today's heavy traffic demands quite a high level of skill, and you don't have much room for error. Today's driving demands a lot of patience and consideration.

As drivers we need to cooperate with each other on the road, to keep the traffic flowing smoothly and ensure road safety. The worst thing that you can do is fall into the trap of thinking that this is a competitive environment. If an eldery lady walks in front of you on the footpath, 99% of people will apologise (even if it was her fault) and help her to pick up her shopping. If the same lady drives out in front of you on the road, why do so many people feel offended, outraged or frustrated?

You might be driving along quite happily at a cruising speed until someone overtakes you, and only then do you get the urge to speed up to keep after them and overtake them in turn if you can. This is a recognisable human tendency, especially for young men, but remember that these are *irrational* reactions. They come from the deep-seated primitive part of our

HINTS & TIPS

If a Garda car patrol wants you to stop for any reason, they will use their flashing blue lights and left indicators. You must pull over and stop (having checked that it's safe by using MSMM); when you stop, switch off your engine.

brains and we have to consciously control them.

There is a psychology to car use that can trick us into anger, irrationality and bad judgement. The first thing to do in countering this is to recognise that it is happening. Imagine a dinner party with your least favourite celebrity or politician as a guest across the table from you. You will not snort in contempt at his or her comments in the same way that you would if you were watching them on television. This is because the complex rules of social interaction – good manners, if you like – prevent you from provoking an aggressive response.

Back inside the car we are in an environment where no threat is felt. We are half way between the dinner party and the TV set. We feel no need to restrain manifestations of aggression; hence we are much more ready to vent feelings of frustration. We are also likely to perceive our car in some sort of territorial way and to seek jealously to protect 'our space'.

Likewise there is a tendency to want to 'get in front'. These urges are throwbacks to our evolutionary heritage. They are not character flaws; in fact they are essential urges for

> ## HINTS & TIPS
>
> You may encounter drivers making unexpected errors when you are near airports and ferry ports. This isn't surprising if they have just arrived from a country where they drive on the right. You will recognise a non-Irish registration plate, but even a 'local' car may be rented and have a bewildered tourist driving it. Be patient, at all times.

successful sports stars and for success in many other walks of life. But we have to make ourselves realise that when we are on the road we are just getting from A to B, and are not in competition.

In the event that the person in the other car is also in belligerent mood the responses can escalate. So the first thing to remember is not to be part of the problem. A gesture that to you is harmless – like the toot of a horn – could be just the provocation needed to push another driver into outright anger. Resolve at the start not to let 'liberty-takers' get to you.

Other drivers are not out to annoy you deliberately; when they make an aggravating move it is almost certainly unintentional. Do not compete or retaliate. If someone's driving annoys you don't try to 'educate' them. Leave it to the Garda.

Be patient and be polite. Others will usually let you in if you signal properly but will resist being forced to do so. Say thanks when you can and apologise if you need to. It is amazing how a small courteous gesture can diffuse traffic anger.

Glaring eye contact, gestures, flashing lights and blaring horns are all worse than useless. They do not speed you up and can be the last straw for someone else.

If you're a learner driver, you hope that others will make allowances for your inexperience. If you're an experienced driver, you can remember what it was like to be a learner, and anticipate that they're sometimes going to stall, or that they may not 'make normal progress'.

HINTS & TIPS

The number of vehicles on Irish roads has grown phenomenally in recent times. In 1990 (our benchmark year for the Kyoto Protocol) there were 1.05 million registered vehicles in the country. By the end of 2006 that figure was over 2.2 million.

So '*consideration* not competition' is the key; here are some suggestions that apply to general driving.

- Don't assume you have priority; and even when you know you do, be prepared to give way if you can see that this is the best way to prevent an accident.
- Always give **clear signals**: in good time, where possible; and cancel the signal when you've finished moving in that direction. (As a driver, you need to know all the arm signals shown in the *Rules of the Road*, so that you can understand the meaning of any arm signals used by another road user, such as a cyclist or person riding a horse, even if you are unlikely to need to use them yourself.)
- When turning right, move into position *in plenty of time* so that other drivers know what you are doing.
- Obey any signals from: **Gardai** **traffic wardens** **school crossing patrols.**
- Where possible, make 'normal progress'.
- Drive at the right speed for the road you're on, *keeping* to speed limits and *adjusting your speed downwards* for bad weather, road works etc.

- *Anticipate* bends, junctions and roundabouts by slowing down in advance. Be ready to change gear.
- Don't weave in and out of **traffic queues** to try and gain a few extra feet.
- *Be aware* of more vulnerable road users (see 'Road users at risk', page 118).
- And finally – remember that *anyone can make a mistake*, or have an off-day!

To sum up: a sense of shared responsibility, not competition, should be uppermost in a driver's mind – and it can even be good for your insurance premiums!

TEST YOUR UNDERSTANDING OF THIS SECTION

1. Why should you be on the look-out for hazards around airports and ferry ports?
2. The indicators on modern cars are very efficient, so why do you still need to learn about arm signals before taking your test?
3. If a Garda car is following you, how will the Gardai let you know if they want you to stop?
4. Why should you avoid gestures like tooting the horn?
5. How should you approach a bend in the road?

ANSWERS ON PAGES 169–70

I'M RIGHT BEHIND YOU!

Drivers closing on you at high speed with headlights blazing, horns blaring and fingers raised in unmistakable gestures – any new driver who's experienced this kind of harassment knows how frightening it can be.

You assume you must have done something wrong, or that the driver behind can see a problem with your car and is trying to draw your attention to it. Unfortunately, in the vast majority of cases it's neither of these; you have simply incurred the wrath of an impatient driver who's letting you know in no uncertain terms that he (or she) wants you to *get out of the way*!

We are back to the problem of evolution again… Even if you're confident that you're in the right place on the road – and driving at the correct speed for the type of road and conditions – the best response is to allow the driver behind to pass you. An aggressive response will do no good and could very well make the situation worse. If a dog barks at you, you don't feel the urge to bark back. Think of ignorant drivers in the same way.

> ### HINTS & TIPS
> Remember the two second rule! If you slow down to give more room between your car and the one in front, you're protecting both yourself and the driver behind.

TAILGATING

Driving excessively close up behind another vehicle is known as tailgating – and it's dangerous.

The car in front may stop suddenly (e.g. to avoid hitting a child or animal that has dashed out into the road); the car following runs the risk of crashing into it (especially if the brakes are faulty).

Rear-end shunts account for a large percentage of all accidents (see 'Motorists with attitude', page 42). In these situations, the driver of the car behind is almost always judged to be the guilty party.

So tailgating can be expensive as well as dangerous. It is also ill-mannered, and can be intimidating for the driver in front.

CHAPTER 3

Another time when drivers are tempted to tailgate is when attempting to pass a large slow-moving vehicle.

However, *keeping well back* improves your view of the road ahead, so that you're better able to judge when it's safe to overtake.

LIGHT-SENSITIVE

In Part 2 we mentioned the habit of some drivers of using headlights and fog lights to intimidate others (see 'Lighting up the night', page 86).

The *Rules of the Road* warns against using lights in any way that could cause discomfort to other drivers. This includes:

- flashing your headlights as you come up behind another car to signal them to get out of the way
- flashing at an approaching motorist in such a way as to dazzle them – this could cause them to lose control temporarily
- using full beam headlights when you should revert to dipped –

HINTS & TIPS

Sometimes glare is due to badly adjusted headlights – or even bumps in the road which make it look as though another car is flashing you.

HINTS & TIPS

When your car is unusually heavily loaded, you may need to make an adjustment to the angle of the headlights.

this can reflect in the rear view mirror of the car in front, making it impossible for the driver to see clearly.

If you are being dazzled by headlights, don't be intimidated, but slow down or stop until you can see to proceed safely. You can also dip your rear-view mirror, i.e. engage its 'night time mode'. This is a simple switch on the mirror that changes its angle and shades the lights from behind. See also 'Fog lights' on page 87 – these rules also apply to driving with fog lights in daylight.

How do I warn other drivers of a hazard ahead?

The *Rules of the Road* tells you not to flash other motorists to warn them of a hazard, although it has to be said, this is what many drivers in fact do. The rule says that you should only flash your lights to let others know you're there.

But it *is* permissible to use your **hazard warning lights**, as follows:
- if your vehicle has broken down and is causing a traffic obstruction
- if you are driving on a motorway or national speed limit dual carriageway and you need to warn other drivers that there's a hazard ahead. But only switch them on for a short time, until you judge that the danger has passed.

Except in the situation described above –
never drive with your hazard warning lights on.

SOUND THAT HORN

Compared with the conventions in some other countries, there are very few occasions when you can use your horn.

It's often wrongly used:
as a form of greeting when you're driving along and see someone you know; or by parents providing a 'taxi service' who want their children to know they've arrived to transport them to their next destination.

But it should be used:
only to let other drivers know you're there (just like the lights, above). Places where you would sound your horn include when you're coming up to a hump-back bridge or a completely blind corner.

In addition, don't sound your horn:
- at horses
- in a built-up area between 11.30pm and 7.00am
- when you're sitting in your car while it's stationary – unless you can see another vehicle heading towards you in a dangerous manner and need to attract the driver's attention.

The horn is an **audible warning signal** and should be kept for dangerous situations only. It is not for expressing opinions about other people's driving!

CHAPTER 3

TEST YOUR UNDERSTANDING
OF THIS SECTION

1. What is meant by tailgating, and why should you avoid doing it?
2. Why could flashing your headlights be a danger to other drivers?
3. When are you allowed to switch on your hazard warning lights?
4. In what situations should you sound your horn?
5. Is it always wrong to sound your horn when the car is stationary?

ANSWERS ON PAGE 170

IT'S NOT ME, IT'S THE OTHERS!

This is a fair point!

It's very annoying to find that, when you've been following some rule of the road to the letter, another driver proceeds to take advantage of your care and consideration. But in today's demanding driving conditions *YOU NEED TO THINK FOR OTHER DRIVERS AS WELL AS YOURSELF.*

Here are some potentially hazardous situations where you could find yourself feeling resentful because of the actions of **other drivers**.

DRIVING AT THE CORRECT SPEED LIMIT

If you're doing 50kph and that's the correct speed limit for the road you're on, what is your reaction going to be if another driver comes up fast behind you, flashing their lights and maybe sounding the horn?

You might react by:
- speeding up to get away from him/her
- deliberately slowing down to annoy the other driver
- adjusting your position on the road so that the car behind can't overtake.

However, the best thing to do is to *let them overtake*, so that you can get on with driving at the appropriate speed in peace.

BEING 'CUT UP' BY OTHER DRIVERS

If you drive regularly, especially on our single carriageway roads, you'll be aware that some drivers take astonishing risks when overtaking; on hills, approaching bends, and in many other places where they cannot possibly see the road ahead far enough to overtake safely.

> ### HINTS & TIPS
>
> Remember that tailgating is dangerous and distracting for the other driver in front. If a crash happens, the driver behind is almost always held to be responsible.

CHAPTER 3

Narrow roads are a feature of Irish life and this is only changing slowly as our road network continues its modernisation. There are long stretches of the primary road network where you just cannot overtake. This means that long queues of impatient cars build up behind slow moving vehicles. As soon as there is any sort of chance to overtake, a lot of drivers instantly want to go for it.

For example, on stretch of road where there is only perhaps a kilometre available for overtaking before the road narrows again, you will often see vehicles speeding along the outside lane to get past the truck while they can.

It's quite understandable that you might feel tempted to:
- accelerate to get up close behind them
- flash your headlights at the truck
- sound the horn for a long time so that they can see that you want to get past.

But again, the best thing is to *let the risk takers get on with it* – and improve your own position by *dropping back so that you can keep the correct separation gap* between you and the truck in front (see 'Stopping distances', page 74).

Of course it is frustrating having to have to wait a few kilometres before your chance comes along, but in reality how much time is it actually going to cost you?

Let us imagine that you really are badly stuck and you must wait behind the truck for another ten kilometres. So for 10km, you will travel at 80kph instead of 100kph. That means that your journey has been lengthened by 1 minute 42 seconds – less time than it takes for the kettle to boil.

Even that overstates the amount of time that you 'lost'. Consider how often you watch a reckless speeder zoom past a truck, only to find that you are just 20 yards behind him ten minutes later when traffic has slowed you both. Clearly, it's not worth taking such a huge risk as to try overtaking without enough room.

DRIVING A SLOW VEHICLE

When you're driving a slow-moving vehicle, especially if it's on a narrow road, or a road with a series of bends, you may become the target for frustration from drivers behind who want to get past.

You might think:

- the safest thing you can do is steer closer to the centre of the road and prevent the cars behind from overtaking, since they won't be able to do so safely
- that it's up to you to wave them on when you can see it's safe for them to overtake
- that you shouldn't wave them on, you should use your left indicator to tell them to go past.

The correct action is to *pull in when you find a safe place* and let the traffic which has built up behind you go past.

HINTS & TIPS

If you are driving past parked cars, it's a good idea to leave as much space as the width of a car door – in case one opens suddenly. If you can't give that much space, slow down so that you could stop if necessary.

SAFETY MARGINS AND YOUR DRIVING TEST

During your test, your ability to judge safety margins accurately will be observed throughout the route. Concentrate on getting used to *judging distances*. How far away is:

- the car behind?
- the car in front?
- the car coming towards you?

Do you have room to overtake safely?

- Before you overtake, use the MSMM routine. It's slightly different for overtaking. Use your mirror to check for following vehicles, then position

CHAPTER 3

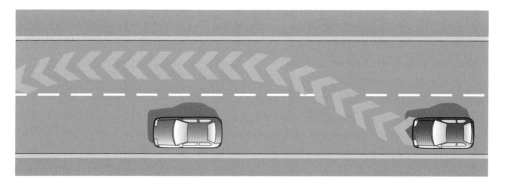

yourself slightly further out than normal to get a view past the vehicle in front. Signal (the driver can see your signal in his or her mirror), then check your mirrors again before moving out to overtake.

- *Don't overtake* if you would have to exceed the speed limit to get past the other car.
- *Yield* if there is an obstruction such as a parked car on your side of the road. (See 'Who goes first?', page 111.) *Be prepared to give way* even if the obstruction is on the **opposite** side of the road.
- *Allow plenty of room* (see the diagram on the previous page) – cyclists and motorcyclists need to be given at least as much room as the width of a car, since they could swerve, and horses even more room in case they bolt.
- Lastly – when you have decided it's safe to overtake, then *be positive about it*; try not to lose your nerve half-way!

But, like all other driving skills, overtaking improves with regular practice as your ability to judge distances improves.

TEST YOUR UNDERSTANDING OF THIS SECTION

1. What should you do if a vehicle is overtaking you when it should not do so?
2. What is the correct way for the driver of a heavy lorry to signal to you that it is safe to overtake?
3. How should you change the 'two second rule' when driving in bad weather?
4. How much room should you allow when overtaking a motorcyclist?
5. Once you have started to overtake another vehicle, what should you do next?

ANSWERS ON PAGES 170–171

HINTS & TIPS

Although you sometimes need to think for other drivers, it's not safe to make decisions for them about when they should overtake.

WHO GOES FIRST?

By now you should be familiar with the rules governing who has right of way. Broadly speaking, traffic on major roads has priority over traffic on minor roads. At roundabouts and in many other situations, you give way to traffic on the right. However there are other traffic contexts and there are other types of road users that you may encounter on the open road. Often you will be required to yield right of way.

A simple way to think about who has priority on the road is that the more powerful gives way to the less powerful. Or, if you've got four wheels you give way to someone who has two, or none at all (i.e. travelling on foot, or on a horse or other beast of burden).

The point here is that just because another type of road user is slower than the majority (cars), it doesn't mean that they don't have priority.

BUT –

of course it's also necessary to give way to other wheeled vehicles when they are large or difficult to manoeuvre: this includes buses, long vehicles, tractors, trams and many more.

Listed on the next pages are some categories of road user that have priority over cars.

Note: this information applies to *non-motorway* roads; vehicles not suited to the higher speeds of motorway traffic are *not allowed on the motorway*. These include motorcycles under 50cc, cyclists, horses, agricultural vehicles and invalid carriages.

CHAPTER 3

HINTS & TIPS

Remember: part of learning to drive safely is being able to control the car at very slow speeds, as when following a cyclist (see 'Can you handle it?', page 17).

PEDESTRIANS

(See also 'Pedestrian crossings', pages 66–7.)

Pedestrians have priority:
- when they have started to cross a road that you want to turn into, *even if there isn't a pedestrian crossing there*
- when they have started to cross on a pelican crossing, *even if the flashing light comes on before they reach the far side*
- when they have stepped on to a zebra crossing. You don't *have* to stop for pedestrians who are standing on the pavement by the beacon but who haven't actually set foot on the crossing; but it's generally accepted that drivers *should* give way to pedestrians waiting to cross. When you're taking your **Driving Test,** your examiner will expect you to stop if there are any pedestrians approaching the zebra crossing who may wish to cross. Show extra consideration to children, elderly people and people with disabilities at pedestrian crossings.

> ### HINTS & TIPS
>
> In some countries, buses and trams have priority over cars – for example, in the Netherlands.

> ### HINTS & TIPS
>
> At an unmarked crossroads, trams always have priority. This is an exception to the rule that no one has priority at an unmarked crossroads (see 'It's in the rules', page 59).

BUSES AND TRAMS

Bus drivers have to rely on motorists giving way to let them pull out after they've stopped to pick up and drop off passengers. So, when you see a bus signalling to pull out, check that it's safe (using MSMM) and then slow down and *give way* to the bus.

You should always give way to **trams,** because they cannot steer to avoid you (see the list of hazards in 'I didn't even see him…', page 56). Don't try to overtake them – especially between the tram tracks and the left-hand kerb, if the trams run in the centre of the road. Take extra care because *trams are sometimes allowed to proceed when you are not* – usually there are traffic signals just for them.

CYCLISTS

It's all too easy for cyclists to become 'invisible' to motorists when driving in busy town traffic; so, try to be aware of cyclists and give way to them.

Cyclists have priority in **cycle lanes** (see 'Other types of lanes', page 66).

They have priority when riding across **toucan crossings** (see page 67) when the lights are in their favour.

You should also *give way* to cyclists crossing in front of you when approaching roundabouts and junctions; and *stay well back* even when they have not yet crossed to the correct lane, since a cyclist intending to turn right may well signal their intention while still in the left lane (see page 64).

HORSES AND LIVESTOCK

When driving past **horse riders**, give them plenty of room; they have priority over cars.

Horse riders, in turn, have responsibilities towards other road users. They must:
- keep to the left
- never ride more than two abreast
- ride in single file when on a narrow road, or approaching a bend.

When driving on country roads there's always a chance of meeting a herd of **sheep** or **cows** (see page 158), so be prepared for this.

As with horses –
- give them plenty of room
- don't sound your horn at them
- stop and switch off your engine until they have moved on.

Note: a person in charge of a herd of animals may signal you to slow down or to stop. Even though this isn't an 'authorised person' such as a Garda, the Road Traffic Act still says that you *must* obey their signal.

CHAPTER 3

HINTS & TIPS

People riding horses on the road are often children, so you need to take extra care; when you see two riders abreast, it may well be that the one on the outside is shielding a less experienced rider.

LARGE VEHICLES

A large vehicle approaching a junction or roundabout may take up a position on the road that would be wrong for a car (see 'Lanes and roundabouts', page 64).

They may keep to the left lane while intending to turn right – or the other way round. They do this because they need extra road space to carry out their manoeuvre, due to their length.

Long vehicles turning into minor roads

A long vehicle that needs to turn left off a major road into a minor road may prepare to do so by moving out towards the centre of the road, or even moving across to the other side.

If you're following them:
- *give way*, and don't try to overtake – on the right or the left
- you might need to slow down and *stop* while the driver of the long vehicle makes the turn.

If you're the one on the minor road, waiting to turn on to a major road:
- don't risk pulling out while the long vehicle is approaching, even if you're turning left and think you've got plenty of time to get out ahead of them
- be aware: there might be a driver speeding along the main road and overtaking the long vehicle; while overtaking they will be hidden from your view. (This can apply to *any* vehicle that masks another – not just to long vehicles.)
- because the long vehicle needs space to manoeuvre when straightening out of its turn, be prepared to clear the junction, or stay well back from it to give the long vehicle more room.

HINTS & TIPS

When following a long vehicle, take a look at the markers on the sides and end. They are there to warn you of the length of the vehicle, and sometimes of overhanging loads.

VEHICLES WITH FLASHING COLOURED BEACONS

As a general rule, give way to vehicles with flashing beacons.

Blue beacons are used by the emergency services, and may not be used by anyone else.
- ambulances
- fire engines
- Gardai
- other emergency vehicles, such as Coast Guard and Mountain Rescue.

As well as beacon lights, these vehicles use flashing headlights or sirens, or both, to alert other drivers. Emergency services drivers have been specially trained, and the law allows them to perform traffic manoeuvres (like travelling through red lights) that are forbidden to other drivers.

NEVER TAILGATE AN EMERGENCY VEHICLE

Green beacons may be used by doctors attending emergency calls.
The way to react when you see a vehicle with a blue or green flashing beacon coming up behind you is to *GET OUT OF THE WAY!*

You have to take care not to cause another accident by your actions, so use your mirrors to anticipate where the emergency vehicle is trying to go, then do your best to make it easier for them to get through. If possible, pull over to the side of the road to let them pass.

Orange beacons are used by:
- accident recovery vehicles
- breakdown vehicles
- gritting lorries and other slow vehicles
- motorway maintenance vehicles
- vehicles with unusually heavy or awkward loads.

Although these are not emergency vehicles, you may need to slow down and give them priority, as they are difficult to manoeuvre.

The flashing orange beacon alerts you to a **hazard**.

CHAPTER 3

GIVING WAY IN NORMAL DRIVING

- At a **junction with a broken white line** across the road, traffic on the major road has priority (see 'Crossing the line', page 71).
- Traffic **on a motorway** has priority over traffic joining from a slip road (see 'Motorway rules', page 92).
- At **roundabouts**, traffic coming **from the right** has priority (see 'Lanes and roundabouts', page 64).
- Where there isn't enough room for two vehicles to pass, due to an **obstruction** such as parked cars, the driver whose side the obstruction is on should give way.
- When driving on **single-track roads** where two vehicles cannot pass side by side, make use of the proper passing places. Don't drive so fast that you can't stop if you meet someone coming the other way; reverse into a passing place if necessary, or stop immediately before one on the opposite side so that the other driver can pass.

(For more tips on country driving, see page 158.)

HINTS & TIPS

Drivers must obey signals given to them by a Garda. These override all other signals and road markings.

- When traffic lights are out of order (see 'Crossroads with traffic lights', page 60) the junction becomes like an unmarked crossroads, so no one has priority. Often drivers will show more care than usual, because they know this is a hazardous situation.

Note: some drivers observe their own rules about who has priority – rules that don't figure in the *Rules of the Road*! You always need to be careful; it will be little consolation to think that you were in the right if there is an accident that could have been avoided.

One of the stereotypes on the road is the old-fashioned male chauvinist. Unfortunately, he does still exist. There are male drivers who believe that they are somehow top of the pecking order and should always have priority, especially when the other driver is female or elderly, and these guys expect to go first at junctions. They get very annoyed if a female driver overtakes them.

There is no logic to this outdated attitude, but the point to remember is that there are times when just acting in accordance with the *Rules of the Road* may not be enough because it assumes that everybody else will do the same. In real life there are plenty of drivers out there who do not obey the rules. They may be just plain bad drivers, or they may be perfectly reasonable drivers who have made an honest mistake.

Nobody is perfect. In fact international research points to a conclusion that whenever a driver makes a decision – when to change lanes or when to emerge from a side road , for example, – one in 500 of those decisions will be a mistake. Whether or not that mistake becomes a tragedy will often depend on others on the road. Hence a good driver is always alert and always expects the unexpected.

TEST YOUR UNDERSTANDING OF THIS SECTION

1. If a car driver is using their indicators to show that they intend to turn into a side road, and there is an elderly pedestrian on the pavement waiting to cross, who has priority – the car or the pedestrian?
2. What should you bear in mind when driving on a road where trams operate?
3. When must you give way to cyclists?
4. Why do you sometimes see horse riders two abreast?
5. Are you required to stop if asked to do so by a person herding animals?
6. How should you react if a long vehicle pulls out towards the centre of the road in front of you when they are signalling to turn left?
7. Why would it not be safe to pull out of a side road if you can see that the vehicle to your left on the main road is intending to turn into the side road?
8. How should you adjust your normal driving when an ambulance with a flashing blue beacon appears behind you?
9. If a traffic light is red but a Garda beckons you forward, what should you do?
10. What sort of vehicle would use flashing blue beacons?

ANSWERS ON PAGE 171

CHAPTER 3

ROAD USERS AT RISK

We've already seen that there are several groups who are more at risk when out on the road than the drivers of cars and other vehicles.
They include:
- cyclists
- motorcyclists
- pedestrians
- horse riders
- learner drivers
- drivers who have recently passed their test
- people with disabilities.

Many road users who are not driving cars have nothing to protect them from the effects of an accident involving a car or any larger vehicle.

Cyclists and people riding motorcycles are more at risk than car drivers because:
- they are affected more by strong winds, or turbulence caused by other vehicles
- they are sometimes difficult for car drivers to see.

PEDESTRIANS MOST AT RISK

Children haven't yet developed a sense of danger on the road, and can't judge how close an approaching car is, or its speed.
They may:
- run out into the road without looking
- appear without warning from between parked vehicles (see 'I didn't even see him...', page 48)
- step into the road behind you while you're reversing – you may not see them behind you because of their size.

People who are unable to see and/or hear

A blind person will usually carry a **white stick** to alert you to their presence.
If the stick has a **red band,** this means that the person is also deaf, so will have no warning of an approaching car either visually or from engine noise.

HINTS & TIPS

In some countries cycle helmets are compulsory, and have been shown to reduce casualties, especially among the young.

Elderly people and others who have difficulty in walking

Some pedestrians need more time to walk across a pedestrian crossing, or to finish crossing a road you are waiting to turn into. *Don't* hurry them or sound your horn, but wait until they have reached the pavement on the opposite side of the road before you drive on (see 'Who goes first?', page 112).

SIGNS THAT ALERT YOU TO ROAD USERS AT RISK

Advance warning of school crossing patrol.

School crossing patrol.

Pedestrians walking in the road ahead (no pavement).

Elderly or disabled people crossing.

Cycle lane and pedestrian route.

Sign on back of school bus or coach.

CHAPTER 3

WALKERS IN AN ORGANISED GROUP

You may have to deal with a large group of people walking together – members of a ramblers' club, or perhaps young people out on a sponsored walk.

There are rules in the *Rules of the Road* that the walkers must follow:
- they should walk on the path if there is one, or otherwise keep to the *left*
- a 'look-out' should walk at each end of the line (carrying a light at night – **white** for the person at the front of the line, **red** at the rear)
- they should be wearing **fluorescent clothing** (reflective at night).

Provided they're doing all that, you should be able to see them in good time; and drive past them slowly and carefully when it's safe to do so, giving them plenty of room.

LEARNER DRIVERS

Some groups of motorists are known to be more at risk of accidents, especially young and inexperienced drivers (see 'Motorists with attitude', page 43).

They may not be so fast at reacting to hazards, and may sometimes make wrong judgements.

In theory, it's easy to spot a learner driver by the 'L' plate; but the reality is that there are a lot of people out there who very foolishly do not comply with the obligation to display one. As we also know, being a fully qualified driver does not guarantee that they will do the correct thing.

DRIVERS WITH DISABILITIES

You may recognise a car driven by someone who's disabled if they display a **disabled driver sign** or parking permit.

This gives them the right to park in a space reserved for drivers with disabilities (see 'Where to park – and where not to', page 78).

Often disabled people drive cars that have been specially adapted for them, but you may also see small powered vehicles with a maximum speed of

---

HINTS & TIPS

You might think that 50kph is a safe speed, but statistics show that 50% of pedestrians hit by a car travelling at 50kph will be killed.

13kph. The orange beacon warns you that there is an unusually slow vehicle on the road.

OTHER DRIVERS AT RISK

How much are you, as a driver, at risk on the road? *In general* – you're far safer *inside* a car than the more vulnerable road users *outside*!

Modern cars are built to extremely high standards of safety, and will withstand impacts more effectively than older models.

For example, SIPS stands for Side Impact Protection System; this means the car is designed to protect you as much as possible in the event of a sideways collision. Many modern cars now have multiple airbags and a host of other features as part of their passive safety engineering.

HINTS & TIPS

In Ireland there are approximately 380,000 drivers who hold provisional licences and have never passed their driving test. Add to that a large number of drivers from outside the jurisdiction who are now working here and it becomes clear that you can never assume that other drivers know the Rules of the Road.

The European New Car Assessment Programme (EuroNCAP) was established in 1997. It's a consortium that includes groups like Europe's motoring organisations (AA Ireland was a founder member), safety research laboratories and some governments. It takes sample models of all new cars and subjects them to independent, realistic crash tests. See www.euroncap.com for more information. Car models are then given safety ratings and the details of the results are published. The good news is that this has made a huge difference to safety standards as manufacturers have competed with each other to get better and better safety scores.

The bad news is that while car occupants are getting the benefits, the pedestrians, cyclists and motorcyclists, who are being hit by cars are not. In recent times EuroNCAP has begun awarding stars for how well cars protect pedestrians in crashes. In the meantime, there is some concern that safer cars may make drivers less worried about driving too fast.

You can help by being aware that:
• if you hit a pedestrian when driving at 60kph, the pedestrian will probably be killed.

CHAPTER 3

- if you hit a pedestrian at 30kph the pedestrian could be killed or injured but stands a far better chance of surviving than at 60kph.

This is the thinking behind plans for the introduction of 30kph speed limits in residential areas. Along with speed humps and other traffic-calming devices, the aim is to reduce accidents in streets where children regularly play, as well as around the entrances to schools.

TEST YOUR UNDERSTANDING OF THIS SECTION

1. Why are cyclists and motorcycle riders described as vulnerable road users?
2. Where should you especially watch out for children in the road?
3. What does a white cane with a red band signal?
4. In what way have the safety features of new cars improved in recent times?
5. What is likely to happen if you hit a pedestrian while driving at 60kph?

ANSWERS ON PAGES 171–172

SHIFT THAT LOAD!

Once you've passed your driving test you'll be entitled to tow a small trailer, or a caravan, behind your car. (To tow larger caravans and trailers, you'll need to take another test.). This is very much an advanced driving skill, and even when the law allows you to tow it is not something that you should undertake lightly. It is also something that most people only do occasionally, and it is easy to be complacent about the extra skill and discipline that is required.

Driving with a load on tow involves:
- being able to call on reasonably advanced driving skills
- distributing the trailer's load correctly
- knowing, and keeping to, the restrictions on how much your vehicle can tow.

The Category B licence that most drivers hold – the 'ordinary' car licence – allows towing within certain restrictions. The trailer, including its load, cannot weigh more than 750kg and cannot be more than half the weight of the towing vehicle. The load must be well secured, and there are other restrictions and stipulations as well. All of these are explained in detail in the *Rules of the Road*.

DRIVING SKILLS NEEDED WHEN TOWING

Towing will affect the way your vehicle handles.
The extra *length* will affect:
- the road space you need to have in order to overtake
- the road position you'll need to take up before making a turn at a roundabout or junction (see 'Large vehicles', page 114).

The extra *weight* will affect:
- how long it takes you to accelerate and pull away
- how much work the engine has to do
- how long it takes you to brake and stop (see 'Stopping distances', page 74).

SO – THINK ABOUT WHAT YOUR STOPPING DISTANCE NEEDS TO BE WITH THE EXTRA WEIGHT.

Common sense tells you to drive more slowly when you're towing. When you are towing a trailer of any sort you are not permitted to travel faster than 80 kph, no matter what the speed limit is, and in most circumstances you should be going more slowly than that.

DRIVING WITH A ROOF RACK

If you've got a roof rack or cycle rack as well as a caravan or trailer it will make an additional difference to the way your vehicle handles. Roof racks even on their own will have an effect on the aerodynamic efficiency of the car, which means that fuel efficiency will not be as good. A roof rack also makes a car more vulnerable to cross winds.

Be aware that a loaded roof rack can add considerable height to your vehicle.

SNAKING

You may have had the experience of driving along a road gasping in disbelief as the caravan in front lurches wildly from side to side behind the car that's pulling it.

So that you don't end up with similar problems, *check*:

• that the load is properly distributed
• that the tow bar is securely attached
• that the coupling height is correct.

What to do about snaking

If you do have to deal with a trailer that starts to snake (weaves from side to side) it means you are probably driving too fast, so lower your overall speed –

• ease off the accelerator, and don't brake
• regain control of the steering
• apply the brakes gently.

Horseboxes

Don't be tempted to drive too fast when you are towing a horsebox. If it starts to snake, use the same technique to regain control.

DISTRIBUTING THE LOAD

If the weight of the load is arranged properly, this should cut down the risk of *snaking*, *swerving* and *losing control*.

Loading a trailer

Load the goods into the trailer with the weight distributed **as evenly as possible** – avoid loading more weight towards the front, or the rear, or to one side.

Loading a caravan – Goods

The technique here is to load any heavy items for the trip

• as low as possible inside the caravan
• mainly over the axles
• safely secured so that they don't roll around.

Loading a caravan – People

There isn't any room for argument here – passengers can't travel in a vehicle that's being towed.

PROJECTING LOADS

It's against the law to have a load on tow that's sticking out in a dangerous manner. It's also a legal obligation to make sure that any load that you are towing is properly secured and is not a danger to others.

If the worst happens and something falls from your trailer while you're on the motorway, or a suitcase falls from your roof rack, remember the correct procedure. Do not attempt to recover it yourself: it is extremely dangerous. Call the Gardai for professional help.

Remember that where there are three or more lanes on a motorway, the outside lane is not available for use by vehicles towing trailers (see page 93). Any vehicle that's towing a caravan or trailer must return to the left lane as soon as possible after overtaking.

CHAPTER 3

PARKING WITH A TRAILER

Take extra care when choosing where to park with a trailer, so that you don't obstruct gates or driveways.

In the next section we'll look at what you can and can't do when carrying **passengers** in your car.

TEST YOUR UNDERSTANDING OF THIS SECTION

1. What difference does towing a caravan or trailer make to the way your car handles?
2. When and why could snaking occur?
3. How should goods be loaded into a trailer?
4. Can you use your caravan to take additional people with you on holiday if there is not enough room for them in the car?
5. What effect will carrying a roof rack have on your vehicle?

ANSWERS ON PAGE 172

IT'S YOUR RESPONSIBILITY

You're responsible for the safety of any passengers who travel in your car.

This is especially important when your passengers include **children.**

It's not easy to control children, especially little ones, and especially when they are confined in one spot for a long car journey. Despite the difficulty, you must try to make it clear that when children are travelling in your car, you expect them to sit still and not to distract you, the driver.

The law makes it quite clear that it's down to **you** to see that any children in your car are wearing their seat belts. If any passenger under 17 is not wearing a seat belt then penalty points are applied to the driver's licence.

HINTS & TIPS

Adult passengers have responsibility for themselves in law, but it makes sense to remind them if you can see they haven't fastened their seat belts. In an accident, passengers in the back who aren't wearing their seat belts could be thrown forward, crushing those in the front seats.

APPROPRIATE RESTRAINTS
Children under 3
• a child seat, or booster seat (the right one for the child's weight)
• a harness
• a baby seat, or baby carrier.

Don't's
Small children *shouldn't* be strapped in using an *adult seat belt*, which could cause them injury and wouldn't be guaranteed to keep them safely seated.

A *lap belt* also should not be used by a child.

You should never allow an adult to sit holding the child on their knee. This is totally unsafe. The forces involved in a car crash, even at relatively low speed, are tremendous. A child will be ripped out of an adult's arms and flung around the inside of a car, with catastrophic results.

Another well-meaning mistake is to put an adult belt around an adult and a small child together. Again, this is extremely dangerous. In a collision the weight of the adult will crush the child against the belt, causing serious injury.

CHAPTER 3

127

You may sometimes have seen one or more children sitting in the back section of a hatchback, i.e. behind the rear seats, while the vehicle is in motion. This is extremely dangerous, and is quite rightly regarded as a serious offence.

Another 'accident waiting to happen' is allowing a child to perch in between the driver's seat and the passenger seat with an elbow on the back of each. This is extremely dangerous. Experienced ambulance crews refer to it as the 'launch' position; children travelling in this way have no protection whatsoever. Even if you don't even have a crash, an emergency braking manoeuvre will 'fire' the child forward into the driver's compartment. This is likely to cause severe injury to the child, and it could also cause the driver to crash.

Children aged 3–11 and under 1.5m (5 feet) tall

• should be strapped in using an appropriate child restraint. Laws introduced across the European Union mean that they require an additional booster seat to ensure that the adult seatbelt fits them appropriately. Full details are explained in the *Rules of the Road*.

HINTS & TIPS

The European Union has laid down minimum requirements which all EU countries have transcribed into local law. This means that the rules relating to children and their seat restraints in cars are the same across the EU.

CHILD LOCKS

These are provided so that the driver can prevent child passengers from accidentally opening the **rear doors**. They are usually activated or deactivated via small switches in the side of the door. See your vehicle's handbook for details of child locks in your own car.

REAR-FACING BABY SEATS

DON'T fit one of these into a *front seat protected by an airbag*.
In a collision it is possible that the back of the baby seat will come within the explosive range of the airbag as it expands, and the impact could seriously injure the baby.

However, modern car design has taken note of this. In many more modern cars there is the facility to turn off the passenger airbag, usually by means of a small key or switch. Your car's manual will have instructions if this facility is available.

TEST YOUR UNDERSTANDING
OF THIS SECTION

1. If a child and his or her parent are travelling in your car, is the parent responsible for the child's safety?
2. What is an appropriate restraint for a child aged under 3 travelling in your car?
3. Under what height must a child use a booster seat?
4. Why is it not acceptable for an adult to hold a small child in their arms in a car?
5. What should you bear in mind when positioning a rear-facing baby seat?

ANSWERS ON PAGE 172

CHAPTER 3

TRUST ME, I'M A FIRST-AIDER

Would you be able to help someone injured in a road accident?
Some people fight shy of giving assistance, on the basis that 'a little knowledge is a dangerous thing', so they might do more harm than good.

BUT – if you can get some basic training and become more confident about being able to give the right kind of First Aid, then it's good news for you and for the accident victim –
• because you'll be better able to cope in the most hazardous situations you'll encounter, making you generally a safer driver.

This section covers First Aid and road accident procedure, gives a summary of what you need to carry in your car, and explains what to do about reporting an accident in which you are involved.

HINTS & TIPS

You can learn the right way to give First Aid. There are classes available from many organisations throughout the country. You can find out more in your local directory or online. It's not difficult and it could save a life.

YOUR FIRST AID KIT

First Aid kits are available from garages and motor accessory stores, and come with their contents already assembled. Either invest in one of these, or make up your own kit, which could include:
• plasters (non-allergenic are safest)
• bandages
• safety-pins
• scissors
• a range of sterile dressings (for burns and other injuries)
• antiseptic wipes (for minor cuts and grazes)
• disposable gloves.
Keep your First Aid kit handy in the car, so you can find it quickly if you need to.

ACCIDENT AHEAD!

Your first warning of an accident on the road ahead will probably be the sound of emergency vehicles, or seeing flashing beacons coming up behind (see 'Vehicles with flashing coloured beacons', page 115).

Slow down and be prepared to **stop** if necessary.

But *don't do so only for the purpose of getting a better look at the accident!* – for example, when you see an accident on the opposite side of a motorway or dual carriageway.

If the emergency services have already arrived, leave them to it and do not stop or delay. Otherwise, stop if you can give assistance, switching on your hazard warning lights (see 'Light-sensitive', page 104).

ACCIDENT PROCEDURE
At the scene of an accident it is important to **assess** the situation first and **check for any danger**. Try to keep a clear head. You must not become a casualty yourself:
- check that no one is smoking
- check that all vehicle engines have been *switched off*
- make sure anyone who isn't injured moves *well away* from the traffic (on a motorway, away from the hard shoulder and central reservation onto the embankment)
- *call the emergency service*s on 999 or 112 if this hasn't been done already, giving full details of location and how many vehicles involved
- don't move anyone who is seriously injured – unless there is a risk of fire or explosion
- **give First Aid** to anyone injured

- **stay** till the emergency services arrive.

FIRST AID
If you are first on the scene and people have been hurt, it can be difficult to know where to start.

It helps to remember the '**ABC**' of First Aid:

A is for Airway
B is for Breathing
C is for Circulation

This tells you what to attend to first when you look at any casualty.

Airway
If an injured person is breathing but unconscious, place them in the recovery position and monitor them carefully for ABC.

If an injured person is not breathing, first make sure nothing is blocking the back of their throat – check for obstructions in the mouth.

Breathing
If clearing the airway has not resulted in the person starting to breathe:
- lift the chin
- tilt the head backwards carefully to open the airway

CHAPTER 3

131

- pinch the nostrils and blow into the mouth until the chest rises
- repeat this every four seconds until the person can breathe unaided, or help arrives.

Circulation

This means bleeding. If a person is bleeding, apply firm pressure to the wound for up to 10 minutes, until the bleeding slows or stops. You can then cover it with a sterile dressing. An injured limb can be raised to lessen bleeding – as long as it isn't broken. In addition to using the 'ABC', you can help by speaking in a reassuring way to the injured person, who is likely to be in shock.

You can try to make them more comfortable and provide a blanket or coat to keep them warm, but avoid moving them unnecessarily, and *DON'T* give them anything to eat or drink.

A question that comes up frequently is: *should you try to remove the helmet from an injured motorcyclist?*

The answer in almost every case is 'NO'.

If you are unfortunate enough to be involved in an accident yourself, here's what to do (provided you are not injured):

- **stop** your car. If you can't pull safely off the road, switch on hazard warning lights and place your warning triangle at a safe distance behind your vehicle on the same side of the road. Take care not to place the triangle where it would cause a hazard.
  Note: never use warning triangles on motorways.
- observe the safety precautions given in 'Accident procedure' above.
- *stand in a safe place* – not between your car and oncoming traffic.

LEGAL REQUIREMENTS – DOCUMENTS

In any accident involving damage to property or to another vehicle, or injury to a person or animal, you must stop and provide the following information 'to anyone with

HINTS & TIPS

Forget about hot sweet tea and anything else that used to be recommended for shock! You must not give an injured person anything to eat or drink – it could delay vital hospital treatment which would require a general anaesthetic.

reasonable grounds for requiring them':
• your name and address
• the name and address of the vehicle's owner, if it isn't you.

Do I have to tell the Gardai?

If anyone has been injured in the accident, then it must be reported to the Gardai.

If no Gardai are at the scene, report the accident to them as soon as possible (*no longer than 24 hours after the accident*); and take documents, including your insurance certificate, to the Garda station within seven days.

It's a good idea to make a record of the events:
• *write down* what happened (noting the time of the accident), sign and date it, and get signatures from other people present if you can – *make a note* of the details of the other drivers involved, and any witnesses

• *draw a diagram* of the position of the vehicles on the road – or take a photograph, if you have a camera with you
• *record* all road markings and traffic signs at and around the scene
• *make a note of the weather conditions* at the time (for example, wet road, fog).

This will come in useful later if you need to make an insurance claim.

What if no one was injured?

'Damage-only' accidents have to be reported to the Gardai only if you were **not** able to give your name and address to any interested parties.

DEALING WITH OTHER PROBLEMS

Although less serious than accidents, there are other unexpected mishaps that can occur during driving, such as burst tyres and punctures.

Burst tyres

If a tyre bursts you will start to lose control of the car. Don't brake suddenly, but pull up slowly when it's safe to do so, keeping a firm grip on the steering wheel. If you can't find a sufficiently safe place to change the tyre yourself, or if you're on a motorway, then call for breakdown assistance.

Punctures

The worst place to get a puncture is, of course, a motorway.

If you do get one:

- pull up on the hard shoulder
- use the emergency phone to call for assistance.

Warning! –

don't ignore any **warning lights** that come on while you're driving. Prompt attention to the problem will minimise the risk of having an accident later.

OTHER EMERGENCY ITEMS

Some other useful items *to keep in the car* in case of emergency are:

- sunglasses
- warning triangle
- fire extinguisher
- torch
- blanket

Other items to carry with you on all journeys *but not necessarily leave in the car* include:

> ### HINTS & TIPS
>
> There are different priorities if the accident involves a vehicle carrying dangerous goods. See your copy of the Rules of the Road for more information.

- insurance certificate
- driving licence
- motoring organisation membership card
- mobile phone
- spare keys
- spare bulbs and fuses
- car manual
- tow rope
- jump leads
- de-icer and scraper (winter)
- sunglasses (summer or winter – snow or low winter sunshine can be dazzling).

> ### HINTS & TIPS
>
> Everyone is familiar with the emergency number 999; but the pan-European emergency number is 112. This works anywhere in the European Union, including Ireland.

TEST YOUR UNDERSTANDING OF THIS SECTION

1. What items should you carry in your car in case someone is injured in an accident?
2. Why is it important that no one smokes at the scene of an accident?
3. What details should you have ready when you call the emergency services?
4. Should your first priority be to pull injured people out of the road?
5. What is the 'ABC of First Aid'?
6. What should you give an injured person to drink?
7. What should you do if you come across an accident where the emergency services are already in attendance?
8. At an accident scene, who is legally allowed to ask for your details?
9. After an accident, how long do you have before you must report it to the Gardai?
10. A motorcyclist has been thrown from his or her bike. Should you remove his or her helmet to help him breathe more easily?

ANSWERS ON PAGES 172–173

TAKING THE TEST – AND BEYOND

APPLYING FOR YOUR TEST

So you have been steadily learning how to drive correctly; you have been trained by proper instructors and have been building up experience in the company of qualified drivers. You have studied your theory and swotted up on your *Rules of the Road*. The only thing that remains to convert your green provisional licence into the pink of a European format 'full' driving licence is to get through that rite of passage that we all go through at some stage: the Driving Test.

The Road Safety Authority is the body that is in charge of driver testing in Ireland, so that is where you need to send your application. Their address is:

Driver Testing Section
Road Safety Authority
Government Offices
Ballina
Co. Mayo

There is a great deal of information on their general website www.rsa.ie and on the specific site www.drivingtest.ie You can apply for the test online (provided you have a valid Laser card, Visa or Mastercard), or you can download the application form and send it by post. You can also pick up the form at Motor Tax Offices, public libraries or Citizens' Information Offices. The fee for Category B (cars) stays the same no matter which way you apply: it costs €38.

To apply to take the Driving Test, you must be normally resident in Ireland and you must have a valid provisional licence in the category of vehicle that you want to be tested for. In most cases that's Category B: ordinary cars or light vans with passenger accommodation for no more than 8 passengers and with a gross vehicle weight of no more than 3,500kg. Other categories are more specialised, and are listed in Chapter 1 (see p21).

CHAPTER 4

HINTS & TIPS

There are approximately 196,000 Driving Tests conducted every year. Of that figure, the failure rate is usually around 45%. It is interesting to note that males have a small but definite advantage and are more likely to pass. This just goes to show that the test is only part of the story as the accident risk for males is statistically far higher.

The Road Safety Authority wants to reduce test waiting times so that nobody has to wait more than ten weeks between sending in their application and sitting the test. Unfortunately that is still an unrealised ambition. There is still an enormous backlog of people who need to do the test, and that means delays. The average waiting time is now 22 weeks, and there are fresh applications being made at the rate of 250,000 per year. It is worthwhile applying for the test as soon as you can and then spending your time while you are on the waiting list learning properly and developing your driving experience.

There is a fine line here. A lot of people make the fundamental mistake of thinking that they are perfectly good drivers because they have been on the road for a year or two, and they neglect proper learning and proper preparation. They are likely to have picked up a whole range of bad and careless habits in this time, and these do not get corrected by one last 'quickie' lesson a few days before the test. They then feel aggrieved and surprised when they fail.

A lot of people do fail first time around. In fact, the pass rate overall is usually less than 55%. This is more than a little sobering and will do nothing to calm the nerves. But if you have done your preparation well, you can consider yourself as being at a very big advantage. Driving testers report that many people fail because of fundamental mistakes that proper training could have avoided.

There are a total of 49 driving test centres in the country. Five of these are in Dublin and the others are spread throughout the country. A full list of these, along with their current waiting times and pass rates, is available at www.rsa.ie. The RSA will try their best to give you an appointment in the test centre of your choice, and you can also specify dates or days when you will not be available. In certain circumstances they will try to give you a faster appointment; for example, if you urgently need a full licence for a job application. This cannot be guaranteed however.

HINTS & TIPS

No matter what conspiracy theorists might believe, there is no 'quota' system for passing or failing drivers. Like it or not, the only reason that your tester has for not awarding you a test pass is if he or she has noted problems with your driving.

You will hear from the RSA in writing about five weeks before your test appointment. This will give you the time and place for your driving test. Make the most of the last few weeks' preparation time!

TEST YOUR UNDERSTANDING OF THIS SECTION

1. How much does the driving test cost?
2. How many test centres are there?
3. How can you best spend your time 'on the waiting list'?
4. What are the disadvantages of doing the test after having been driving for a year or more?
5. Roughly what percentage of people who attempt the test are successful?

ANSWERS ON PAGE 173

CHAPTER 4

WHAT HAPPENS ON 'THE DAY'?

It's understandable that you might feel rather apprehensive when the day of your test comes round – after all, you've invested a lot of time and money in preparing for it, and passing it is an important step.

HOW TO PREPARE YOURSELF

Most people feel more confident if they're reasonably smartly dressed on the day of their driving test; and of course, it's important to wear comfortable shoes.

CHECKING OUT THE CAR

If you are taking your test in the driving school's car, make sure that it is one that you are familiar with and comfortable with. Your instructor should have made sure the requirements concerning the car have been complied with. Whether the car is yours or the driving school's you must be sure of the following:

- seat belts in good condition
- head restraints in correct position
- rear-view mirror in correct position
- mechanically sound
- roadworthy, with NCT certificate if necessary (see 'Are you legal?' on page 24)

- current tax, insurance and NCT disk (if applicable) displayed
- 'L' plates displayed
- fully insured for you to drive.

You should arrive at the test centre in good time. Have an extra ten minutes or so in hand to avoid being in a rush. Try to be relaxed; the calmer your state of mind, the more likely you will be to drive smoothly.

After confirming your name and address, the first thing the tester will do is check that your provisional licence (a) is current, (b) is for the correct category, and (c) relates to you. Assuming that everything is in order, you will then be asked to read and sign a statement which says that your vehicle is roadworthy and that you have proper insurance.

Needless to say, you should have checked all of these things beforehand. Ideally have all of your material ready days in advance. It won't do you any good to be frantically searching for your provisional licence on the morning of the test. Unfortunately if you haven't got all of your details and your car in good order then you will not be able to continue with the test, and you will forfeit both your fee and your place in the queue.

All these details attended to, it is time at long last for the driving test itself…

The driving test will last between 40 and 45 minutes. There are three distinct sections. These are:
The Oral Test
The Technical Checks and Secondary Controls
The Drive

Almost everyone says that the first two are very easy, and because of the way the scoring system works, if you do fail it will be because of what happens on the drive. But we will take them each in turn.

THE ORAL TEST

The tester will ask you a number of questions which are based on the *Rules of the Road*, and ask you to identify a number of road signs from a sign card. You will be expected to know what they mean and to understand the regulatory and warning signs as described in Chapter 2. You may also be asked a question or two about on the road situations, a little bit like having an oral version of one

or two questions from the Driver Theory Test. It won't be difficult but it does mean that you need to know your *Rules of the Road*.

At the car, the tester will inspect the tax disc, insurance disc, 'L' plates, and NCT disc (if one is required) to ensure that they are in order. The tester will also check that the brake lights and indicators are working properly, and that there are no obvious defects with the vehicle.

THE TECHNICAL CHECKS AND SECONDARY CONTROLS

There are ten technical checks that you should know how to perform, and the tester will ask you to explain or demonstrate three of them. The technical checks are:
(a) tyres, (b) lights, (c) reflectors, (d) indicators, (e) engine oil, (f) coolant, (g) windscreen washer fluid, (h) steering, (i) brakes, (j) horn.

If, for example, you are asked how you would check the tyres, you can explain verbally that you would visually inspect each tyre in turn for air pressure, defects, or damage, and that you would check that the tread depth is not less than 1.6mm.

CHAPTER 4

If you are asked how to check the engine oil, you can explain verbally about the procedure for taking out the dipstick, cleaning it to ensure a good reading, replacing it and withdrawing it again so that you can see that the oil level is between the maximum and the minimum. You may well be asked to open the bonnet to point out the dipstick, coolant, windscreen washer, brake fluid, or power assisted steering fluid reservoirs, and close it again securely, so make sure that you know how to do this on whatever car you are using.

Demonstrating the technical controls

This is even easier. The list includes (a) temperature control, (b) fan, (c) air-vents, (d) rear window heater, (e) wipers, (f) windscreen washer, (g) light switches, (h) air intake control, (i) front and rear fog lights, and (j) air conditioner (if fitted). The tester will sit in the car with you and will ask you how to work three of the controls, such as the windscreen washer, the rear window heater, the lights or foglights. He or she will also ask you to ensure that the seat, seat belt, and mirrors are properly adjusted, and that the doors are properly closed.

THE DRIVE

The tester will then instruct you to start the drive. They will be formal at this point, and there will be no additional or unnecessary conversation while the driving aspect of the test is going on. This doesn't mean that they don't like you! They don't want to distract you from your driving. You can ask the driving tester to repeat or explain any instruction that you do not understand, but remember to concentrate on your driving and do not try to impress with how relaxed and chatty you are.

A handy tip is that you should reverse into a parking space when going for your test; otherwise the very first thing that you will have to do is reverse the car out.

After that, it's a case of driving along normal roads following the directions of the tester. The roads are selected so as to provide a range of different conditions and a varied density of traffic, and suitable areas are chosen for you to carry out the set exercises.

You will be given a simple instruction like: 'When you are ready, I would like you to move off and proceed straight ahead please.' You will also hear instructions like 'I would like you to take the next left/right,' or 'I would like you to take the third exit off the roundabout' or 'I would like you to pull in on the left somewhere safe and convenient please.'

In all cases, remember what you have learned. You will be checking your rear view mirror regularly as a matter of course. Whenever you get an instruction, remember the procedure:

Mirror – check your rear view and then side mirrors
Signal – indicate as appropriate
Mirror – check the mirrors and blind spot again before you move the car out of the lane
Manoeuvre – perform the manoeuvre smoothly.

When you are travelling along the road you will be expected to make 'normal progress' without undue hesitation, including at junctions and roundabouts. This means that you cannot travel so slowly that you are causing frustration to traffic behind you. More obviously, you cannot drive so fast that you are breaking the speed limit or are at risk of not being able to react to a hazard.

Throughout the test, the tester will be assessing:

• whether you are competent at controlling the car
• how you react to any hazards that occur in the course of the test
• whether you are noticing all traffic signs and signals, and reacting in the correct manner.

You should normally drive in the centre of the lane that you are on, but remember to leave plenty of clearance for cyclists. If you are passing parked cars then you need to be careful to allow space in case the doors open. This may mean indicating to the right and moving to the right; remember to return smoothly to the correct position after you have passed the hazard.

The test has a number of compulsory manoeuvres that the tester will instruct you to carry out. You will have been taught these by your instructor and you will have practised them.

These are: moving off, (including on a hill), turning left, turning right, stopping, reversing around a corner, turnabout, and parking. In all cases, the tester will be assessing your control of the vehicle and your safety awareness. You must maintain the car's position correctly, you must maintain good observation (do not neglect your mirrors), you must signal clearly and appropriately, and you must demonstrate that you understand the concept of 'right of way' in interaction with other traffic.

Moving off

Check your mirrors and signal right. Select first gear and find the contact point of the clutch. Check your blind spot and be prepared to yield to approaching traffic. Release the clutch and move smoothly into the traffic flow. On a hill start, use the handbrake to ensure that the car does not roll back.

Turning left

Check your rear view and left side mirrors. Signal left. Assume a position as far to the left of the lane as is practical. Select second gear on approaching the corner. Check mirrors and blind spot once again, then turn your steering wheel to the left making sure that you do not over-steer or under-steer. Do not allow your hands to cross over each other. Do not hit or mount the kerb, and do not swing wide. Straighten smoothly when you are around the corner.

What if there had been a cyclist coming up on the left? Would you have seen them? What if a pedestrian had walked out at the corner? Did you have time to stop safely? If the answer is 'no', that is a dangerous fault.

Turning right

Check your rear view and right side mirrors. Signal right. Take up a position just to the left of the centre of the road. Select second gear on approaching the corner. You may well have to stop if traffic is approaching as they will have right of way. Judge their speed and distance. Check the mirrors again, and it is critical that you check your blind spot over your right shoulder, before you turn the wheel. Do not turn into the corner until the front of your car can clear the centre line of the road that you are turning into; in other words, do not cut the corner – you should not need to encroach on the oncoming lane of the road that you are turning into. Remember also not to go too far past the correct turning point, which would mean you had to 'swan-neck' back into position.

What if there had been a motorcyclist approaching on your right? Would you have seen them before you turned your steering wheel?

Reversing around a corner to the left

Your car should be within 45 centimetres of the kerb when you pull in on the left. When asked to reverse around the corner, remember that MSMM applies to every manoeuvre. Check your mirrors and blind spots. Reversing is a situation in which you are allowed to remove your seat belt, but that can be little more than a distraction. It is an old-fashioned rule that dates back to a time when seat belts were manually adjusted and could be awkward when looking back over your shoulder. It's probably best to leave it on; at least that way you won't forget to put it back on afterwards.

Select reverse, come to the contact point of the clutch, check mirrors and blind spots again, and begin to move slowly. When the back of the car reaches the start of the corner, start turning the wheel to the left. This is a tricky manoeuvre that you should practise thoroughly. Make sure that you do not either hit the kerb or stray too far out from it. During the reverse, check carefully all around for children, pedestrians, cyclists, and other traffic, and stop, if necessary. Keep reversing until the tester tells you to stop or until you reach an obstacle.

Did you control the car smoothly? Did you check your mirrors? Would you have seen a hazard?

Turnabout

This used to be called the 'three point turn' but in fact you do not need to complete it in three moves; it can just as easily be a five point turn provided that each phase is treated as a separate manoeuvre and that you remember MSMM for each one.

The tester, still in formal mode, will give you an instruction something like this:
'I would like you to turn your car around on the road to face the opposite way. You may go over and back more than once if necessary.'

As before, check all round, including mirrors and blind spots. Indicate right. Check mirrors again, then move. As soon as the car is in motion, turn the wheel to the right. When you are approaching the kerb on the other side of the road, start turning the wheel back to the left. It's usually about right to start turning the wheel when the kerb has disappeared from your view as the bonnet obscures it; again, this is something to have practised. Just before you reach the kerb, slow the car to a stop.

CHAPTER 4

Treat the next phase, reversing, as a separate manoeuvre. However, on this occasion no signal is required. Check all around you, engage reverse, check around you again, then commence reversing, turning the wheel to the left while continuing to watch all around. When you are close to the opposite kerb, stop the car smoothly.

For the next phase, you are in first gear again. On this occasion check mirrors and blind spots, but in particular look along the road both to the left and right, and when it is clear, commence moving, steering to the right as rapidly as you can do in safety. Remember to keep observing, and to steer without crossing your hands. If you still do not have enough clearance to make the turn comfortably, then repeat the reverse manoeuvre; this is perfectly acceptable.

When you have completed the turn continue straight ahead unless instructed otherwise.

Did you control the car smoothly? Did you maintain continuous observation? Would you have noticed a hazard, like a child's football rolling out onto the road?

The turnabout is in many ways the most complex manoeuvre, and this is where proper lessons pay off. If you were taught by a relative, he or she is very likely not to have understood exactly what the driving tester will be checking for. It is about observation, safety, judgement, control, and smoothness. It is not primarily about skill.

Hand signals

At some point during the test, usually after the reverse or turnabout, the tester will ask you to demonstrate the hand signals which are shown in the *Rules of the Road*.

Parking

This is the last manoeuvre in the test, and it should not be too demanding. You are not formally required to 'reverse park' in the test, but where it is the only option, you should be quite capable of doing it. Real life requires you to do this all the time so you should be well practised. You simply need to drive the car carefully into the parking space back at the test centre and bring it to a smooth stop, signalling as necessary and keeping constant observation.

Despite only taking half an hour, that was probably exhausting! Did you control the car smoothly? Did you remember MSMM?

HOW IS THE TEST SCORED?

During your driving test, the driving tester will be taking note of all aspects of your driving. He or she will be looking for and noting any errors that you make.

There are three grades of 'fault' that are noted. There are Grade 1 faults which are minor, Grade 2 faults which are more serious, and Grade 3 faults which are dangerous or potentially dangerous.

Grade 1 faults do not affect the result of the test. You should try to avoid them, of course, but they are not serious. An example would be not knowing how to perform one of the technical checks.

If you have a total of 9 or more Grade 2 faults overall then you have failed the test. If you have 6 or more Grade 2 faults under the same heading or 4 Grade 2 faults for the same aspect then this too means that you have failed. So if, for example, you do a very good and safe drive overall but you are persistently out of position when turning left, then unfortunately you will fail, and will be told what you need to work on for next time. Grade 3 faults are dangerous, and even one means that you have failed.

Not stopping at a stop sign, failing to stop at a red traffic light, being dangerously out of position on the road, not checking your blind spots; these are all examples of Grade 3 faults.

Once you have parked the car, the tester will not give you your result immediately. He or she is not trying to keep you on tenterhooks, but there is a set procedure that has to be followed. You will be asked to come back to the desk where he or she first asked you your oral questions, and at that point you will be told whether you have passed or failed.

TEST YOUR UNDERSTANDING OF THIS SECTION

1. What documents will your tester check on the day?
2. What pictures will the tester show you as part of the oral test?
3. How many technical checks will you be asked to explain or demonstrate?
4. What does 'normal progress' mean?
5. What are the reversing manoeuvres used in the test?
6. What will the driving tester look for in your general driving?
7. Are you expected to drive without making any mistakes in order to pass?
8. Why should you not cut the corner when turning right?
9. What type of fault will mean an immediate test failure?
10. How long does the driving test last?

Answers on page 173

PASSED?

PASSED?

Good news! Your tester will present you with a 'Certificate of Competency', and you now have most of the privileges of a fully licenced driver. This means that you can drive any vehicle up to 3.5 tonnes gross vehicle weight (assuming that it was the Category B test that you were doing), and you are free to drive on your own without 'L' plates.

However, you still cannot (a) drive on a motorway, (b) tow a trailer, (c) act as an accompanying driver for another learner, (d) drive outside the country, including in Northern Ireland, or (e) carry any passenger for reward, until you obtain the full licence.

However exhilarated you feel about having passed, you'll find it useful to know where your weaknesses lie, so that you can concentrate on improving

HINTS & TIPS

Just because you have passed your test does not mean that you can forget all the 'fussy' things your instructor taught you. It is just as important to drive correctly. Do not strip off your good driving habits with your 'L' plates!

HINTS & TIPS

If you applied for a first provisional licence in the period 25 April 2001 to 10 June 2001, you must submit a theory test certificate with your driving licence application, unless you have already submitted such a certificate. Further information may be obtained on the Driver Theory Test website at www.dtts.ie

those aspects of your driving in the future. The tester will give you a copy of the report showing any faults you made during your test.

Remember also that no-one becomes a perfect driver after a 40-minute test. Everyone on the road needs to concentrate at all times, and in our first years we all get better and safer with experience. Accident statistics show that newly qualified drivers continue to be high risk, so don't make the mistake of thinking that passing the test means that you can relax.

Remember also to let your insurance company know that you have your full licence – you might hear some good news from them.

CHAPTER 4

FAILED?

Disappointing, certainly, but not the end of the world – many people don't pass their first test, but then sail through a second or third, having built on the experience of what it's like to take a test. As we have noted, the overall pass rate is not much better than 50/50. You will probably feel more relaxed next time, helped by the knowledge that you've had more practice in those areas of driving where you weren't sufficiently skilled before.

In explaining the reasons for your failure, the driving tester will present you with a copy of your Driving Test Report Form. This document will give you a detailed breakdown of where you went wrong. The tester is on your side and is willing to help you. You should listen to any advice that you are given and concentrate on those areas in order to be ready for the next time.

TEST YOUR UNDERSTANDING OF THIS SECTION

1. What will the driving tester hand to you on completion of your test if you have passed?
2. Up to what size vehicle can you drive having passed your Category B test?
3. Why is it useful to pay close attention to the driving tester's feedback even if you have passed?
4. After what age can a driver only apply for a three year licence?
5. Does passing your test prove that you are a safe driver?

ANSWERS ON PAGES 174

HINTS & TIPS

Older drivers can apply for a licence that will expire when they reach 70 years of age. Drivers aged 67 or older may apply for a three year licence.

APPLYING FOR YOUR FULL LICENCE

Assuming that you are under 60 years of age, and assuming that you are normally resident in Ireland, your Certificate of Competency means that you can now apply for a 10-year driving licence. Most people want to do this straight away, but you should note that if you delay for more than two years, your Certificate of Competency is no longer valid, which would be a shame after all the trouble that you went through to get it!

Your driving licence is obtained from your local Motor Tax Office. It's a very similar process to getting your provisional licence as described in Chapter 1, except that this time you enclose your Driving Test pass certificate instead of your Theory Test one.

The form that you need is called Form D.401, and as before it is available from public libraries, motor tax offices and Garda stations, as well as being available to download online via the motor tax section of your local authority's website. You must fill out the form and return it with two passport-sized photographs (signed on

the reverse), your Certificate of Competency and your provisional licence. As before, there are certain medical conditions which require a medical report. If you think this might apply to you, you can find out about them on the Department of Transport's website at www.transport.ie.

You also need to enclose the fee, which is €25.

HINTS & TIPS

Checklist

Your application for a driving licence should include in all cases:

• a completed application form (D.401)
• two photographs (signed on reverse)
• your current or most recent driving licence and/or provisional licence
• the appropriate fee
• a Certificate of Competency, if you have recently passed a Driving Test.

and, if required in your case

• a medical report
• declaration re lost/stolen licence (Form D8A)
• Driver Theory Test Certificate.

ADVANCED DRIVING SKILLS – WHO NEEDS THEM?

Passing the Driving Test is not like taking the stabilisers off your bike. The skills learner drivers are taught in the course of their lessons are not intended to be 'only for learners'. They sum up the way good drivers behave at all times. The worst mistake is to think that now that you have a full licence, things like holding the wheel properly or obeying the 'two second rule' are no longer important.

Driving is unusual among practical skills in that, once they've passed their test, most people make no further attempt to improve their driving. Compare the way you approach any other hobby, or craft, or skill that you participate in regularly.

You'd expect to work at improving your skills so that in time you'd become an expert.

But in driving, people seem to assume that *everyone's an expert from the moment they pass their test*!

HINTS & TIPS

Any experience you can get of driving in new conditions or in different kinds of vehicles is valuable in building confidence, and will help to make you a better driver.

MOTIVATION

It's true that at present there is little to motivate people to improve their driving skills.

Research shows that about 35% of young drivers can be classed as unsafe, not because they don't know how to drive properly, but because they choose not to do so after they have passed their tests.

You might gradually start to make changes to the way you drive after a series of **near-misses** (see 'Motorists with attitude', page 46).

But it's possible to plan for improvement in a less risky, more methodical way, just as part of your day-to-day driving.

IMPROVING DRIVING STANDARDS FOR YOURSELF

Think of a routine journey that you carry out frequently.

Next time you're on that route, check the following points:
- Are you driving at the correct speed for the road?
- Are you keeping to the two second rule?
- What are the places where you know you might meet a hazard?
- Are there any traffic signs you're not sure of?

Based on what you observe, make any necessary adjustments to your *road position* and *speed*.

Think about lane use and signalling at roundabouts and other junctions. Are your intentions always clear to other road users?

Start to *anticipate* regular hazards.

For example, if you know that a large concrete lorry usually pulls out of a particular junction every day, be prepared to slow down well in advance.

Make up some extra imaginary hazards and work out how you would respond to them.

If you've found any traffic signs you're not sure of, look them up in the *Rules of the Road*.

To sum up: try to *monitor your own standard of driving*, and see what you could do to improve it.

You could also consider taking an advanced driving course. There are quite a few available, notably those provided by the **Institute of Advanced Motorists (IAM)**.

You'll find details of groups in your area in the telephone directory.

CHAPTER 4

HINTS & TIPS

If you're driving some distance alone, always tell someone else where you're going and when you expect to arrive. This is a useful safety precaution. Also, be sure to carry a mobile phone so that you can call for help in the case of a breakdown or emergency, but don't use it while driving.

THRILLS WITHOUT SPILLS

If you'd like to try your hand at some fast driving in a safe environment, there are motorsport courses where you can be trained and have the experience on an enclosed circuit. This is far better than trying to be a stunt driver on the public roads!

You can also book some practice on a skid pan to find out how it feels when you have to control a skidding car. Your driving instructor or the AA can point you in the right direction.

TEST YOUR UNDERSTANDING OF THIS SECTION

1. Why do people view driving differently from the way they view other practical skills?
2. How can you improve your own standards of driving after you pass your test?
3. How would you find out about an advanced driving course?
4. What precautions should you take when setting out to drive for a long distance on your own?

ANSWERS ON PAGE 174

BUYING YOUR FIRST CAR

This is going to represent a major financial commitment on your part, so of course you'll be keen to get it right.

Fortunately there's a wide range of resources you can draw on for advice, including:

- a local dealer or garage with a reputation for reliability
- general or specialist magazines, and features in newspapers
- the internet; websites like www.drive.ie or www.cbg.ie are very good sources of information.

So before you make your purchase – **do some research!**

HINTS & TIPS

AA Technical Services carries out detailed and meticulous inspections prior to purchase. Fully qualified engineers check the car from bumper to bumper and top to bottom, checking for problems under 175 separate headings. The cars are road tested, and the engineer then produces a clear written report. The service does cost money; depending on the car it is in the region of €350, but skimping on the cost can be a false economy in the long run.

THE RIGHT CAR FOR YOU

You'll need to spend some time thinking about what kind of car you need.

- Would you prefer a manual or automatic gearbox? (See 'Can you handle it?', page 19.)
- Are you likely to want to tow a trailer? (See 'Shift that load!', page 123.)
- How many passengers do you need space for?
- Do you do most of your driving in town? If so, a small car that's economical on fuel is best.
- Or do you drive long distances in the country and on motorways?

BUYING A NEW CAR

Buying a new car is a serious financial commitment. The first thing to consider is depreciation as cars lose their value very quickly. In fact, with some exceptions, they experience their greatest single drop in value the moment they leave the showroom. This is because whoever buys the car next will not be the first registered owner. Cars generally drop to 10% of their original value within 8 years. Imagine if house prices did the same!

CHAPTER 4

155

The very best way to buy a new car is with cash; that way you get the best of any discounts. Car dealers will negotiate on price, so don't be afraid to press them. You are not tied to one dealer nor to one model of car, so you are in a position of strength.

Most people have to get financing of some sort, and the market is full of advertisements and offers from finance houses and others all offering the best deals. AA Finance is included in this.

No matter whom you choose, remember to shop around. The car dealer will almost certainly have a finance deal to offer you, but don't be too easily persuaded. It may be good value but do your research. It is worth checking out www.financialregulator.ie and looking at the price comparison surveys that they carry out.

Think also about how much the car is going to cost you to run. Things like servicing, insurance, fuel and spare parts all add up. A new set of tyres is typically needed every 48,000 kilometres, or every three years.

The AA website, www.AAireland.ie, has detailed information under 'Cost of motoring'.

BUYING A SECOND-HAND CAR

Second-hand cars can be excellent value. For every new car that is sold in Ireland there are 2.5 second-hand cars sold, so clearly hundreds of thousands of motorists make good purchases. But there are pitfalls. Having a professional inspection carried out is relatively inexpensive and could save you a great deal of money.

Unfortunately many second-hand car buyers don't bother. It can be easy to fall in love with a car on a forecourt and rush to purchase, parting with thousands of euros in what is essentially a leap of faith. It pays to be more cautious.

The AA advises car buyers to use reputable dealers. **SIMI** registered dealers are part of a network which includes a complaints arbitration system should things go wrong.

HINTS & TIPS

AA Finance offers a flexible rate car loan which has some very good advantages. It allows you to make early payments to reduce the loan without penalty, and the rates are very good.
Contact 1890 794794 or see www.AAireland.ie for more information.

A reputable dealer is also likely to be able to provide more in the way of after sales service. Private sales can work out well, but there is less protection for the buyer and as always the old saying *caveat emptor* applies.

You can also look for cars sold under the **AA Autocheck** banner. AA Autocheck is a quality assurance scheme for used cars. Dealers undertake to perform a very detailed inspection designed by the AA, and the AA then monitors the dealer to see that standards are kept high.

More information on AA Vehicle Inspections can be found at www.AAireland.ie, or by contacting AA Technical Services at 01 6179370.

TEST YOUR UNDERSTANDING OF THIS SECTION

1. What considerations do you need to bear in mind when choosing your first car?
2. Why could it be a good idea to buy a second-hand car?
3. What running costs should you consider when you are getting a car?
4. What safeguards are available to you if you buy a used car from a dealer?

ANSWERS ON PAGE 174

CHAPTER 4

ALONE AT LAST!

It can come as quite a shock to realise that you are now legally able to drive on your own, with no instructor or 'supervisor' beside you.
IN FACT – IT CAN BE QUITE SCARY!

Driving on a motorway for the first time can be a daunting experience (see 'Motorway rules', page 92). In particular, the techniques for joining and leaving a motorway, lane use and overtaking are different from anything you might have experienced up to now. As mentioned before, motorways are statistically very safe, but then that assumes that everyone who uses them is fully licenced and knows what they are doing. As of now, that includes you!

Take your time to get used to the motorway experience. Do not feel that you have to travel at the maximum speed; think more in terms of comfortable cruising.

OUT IN THE COUNTRY

When you've passed your test you can start discovering some very different kinds of roads from the residential streets that most people become familiar with while they're learning.

You'll have to negotiate **narrow lanes** in remote areas, where visibility is difficult and consideration for other drivers a must.

On single-track roads, passing places usually provided; although in remote areas they may just be gateways to fields. If you do meet another car, try to be co-operative.
If there's a driver coming towards you, or you can tell that the driver behind is anxious to overtake:
• pull into a passing place on your left
• or wait just before a passing place on your right.

Whenever possible, give way to farm vehicles. A tractor and trailer is far harder to manoeuvre out of the way than a car. You may find yourself having to reverse back a bit to get out of its way. And of course, don't park in a passing place.

Be especially watchful for hazards on country roads, since some of the most remote places are also the most beautiful, and there may be large numbers of sightseers around who are not watching the road.

Slow down for bends – they may be sharper than you think – and be on the look-out for concealed junctions.

GETTING AROUND

If you are heading off to an area you don't know well, plan the route in advance and take a good up-to-date road map with you. You can print off a detailed route between any two points in Ireland (or Britain or the Continent) from the AA's website at www.AAireland.ie.

If you're travelling with a passenger, get him or her to navigate for you (but be aware that not everyone is a practised map-reader at first).

And if you're on your own try to have a good idea of your route before you set off. Needless to say, stop the car safely before trying to read the map!

AVOIDING A BREAKDOWN

A breakdown is never a pleasant experience, especially if you are on your own. It can be especially threatening for women as they can feel very vulnerable. Although it may happen without warning, there are things that you can do to minimise the risk of finding yourself stranded.

Keep your car in good working order. Check the oil, battery and the tyre pressures regularly. Don't let your fuel tank run close to empty – keep it well topped up.

Make sure your spare wheel is in good condition. Consider an automatic latex puncture repair aerosol to get you to the nearest garage.

Carry a set of jump leads, some basic tools and a torch.

CHAPTER 4

HINTS & TIPS

At 80 milligrammes, Ireland's drink drive limit is currently one of the highest in Europe, along with the UK and one or two others. Most of the Continent has a limit of 50 milligrammes, and some are even lower. All countries treat drink driving as a serious offence, and being a tourist is no defence.

IF YOU HAVE A BREAKDOWN

You should be a member of the AA. This means you can call a Freephone number for reliable help 24 hours a day, no matter where you are. When giving your details to the Rescue Centre be prepared to tell them exactly where you are and the details of what happened to the car.

If possible, stop the car in a well-lit spot as close to a public phone as is practicable. Keep going until you can stop in the best place. Your safety is of paramount importance, not your car.

Have your mobile phone with you and make sure that it has credit. Mobiles are excellent in these situations because you do not have to go looking for help from strangers. You can stay secure in your car until help arrives.

If you have to stop on the motorway hard shoulder the AA recommends that you leave the car. The AA's experience shows that a very high proportion of motorway accidents involve vehicles parked on the hard shoulder; in this situation, drivers are at risk of being approached or harassed. Stay out of the car with the passenger door open and all other doors locked. This means you can secure yourself inside the vehicle

quickly if you feel threatened. If you are on a secondary or minor road you should remain in the car with all of the doors locked.

Be very careful accepting help from a garage mechanic who has not been sent by the AA and always check their credentials thoroughly. Talk to them through a closed window until you are sure they are who they claim to be. If you do decide to accept help, take a note of the registration number and colour of the vehicle which stopped, and leave those details in your car before you get out.

If stranded, be very careful about accepting a lift.

INCIDENTS

If you see an incident or an accident, or if someone tries to flag you down, think first:

• Is it genuine?

• Could you help?

It is often safer to report what you have seen by phone.

DRIVING ABROAD

The Irish driving licence is acceptable anywhere in the European Union and in most non-EU European countries. If you are venturing as far as the countries of the former Soviet Union or the Balkans then you should have an **International Driving Permit** (IDP) as well.

An IDP is recommended for the US. Some states will accept an Irish licence and some won't, and often car rental companies will insist on it. It is an easy document to obtain: once you have your Irish licence you can get an IDP from the AA at a cost of €5.08.

Driving abroad can be a daunting experience. The most obvious difference is that in most parts of the world people drive on the right. This is certainly off-putting. We have almost all had the experience of being a pedestrian abroad, and even that can be scary when you automatically look in the wrong direction.

HINTS & TIPS

In Sweden they used to drive on the left. They switched in 1967, and it proved to be an enormously complicated and difficult transition. It's highly unlikely that Ireland will attempt it any time soon!

This is even more true as a driver. You have to double and treble your level of concentration, so driving is more tiring. It appears that most people do not have a problem on the first or second day. People tend to be very cautious and just follow the car in front when coming out of an airport or ferry port.

The bigger danger comes later on, as you get more confident. Then one morning you drive out of the hotel gate and instinctively look in the wrong direction. The lesson is never to drop your guard.

RESPECT LOCAL LAWS

In fact quite a few of our Continental neighbours have some unusual laws on their statute books, and most of them are far better at enforcement than the casual Irish.

In Germany, for example, it is a statutory offence to make obscene or derogatory gestures while driving, so watch your road rage tendencies. In Austria tourist access to some areas may be restricted when air pollution levels get too high, and they will not let your car through.

In several countries it is compulsory to carry a warning triangle and a First

CHAPTER 4

HINTS & TIPS

Ireland, the UK and Malta are the only European countries to drive on the left. However there are others across the globe. The formerly British countries of Australia, New Zealand and South Africa are the same. India, with its enormous population, drives on the left and so, very significantly, does Japan.

Aid kit, and of course you will always need an IRL sticker. If you are staying in the EU then you do not need an International Driving Permit. However, it is still worth having one, as some hire companies insist on them.

INSURANCE

Insurance is really the one thing that cannot be overlooked. Breakdown insurance is a must. Breaking down abroad is usually inconvenient and always costly. For example, it can cost as much as €3,000 to recover a car from Spain to Ireland. French labour charges can be €35 per hour.

If you break down on a British motorway you will need to be covered by a motoring organisation. Your Irish AA membership will entitle you to service, but if you are not a member of any rescue service then be prepared to pay a hefty bill – in the region of £100

– just to be towed off the motorway by the garage that the police will detail to get you clear.

It is important to notify your insurance company that your vehicle is being taken out of the country. If you do not, you could find yourself with just the legal minimum third-party cover abroad even if your insurance is comprehensive here. You should also bring the car tax book with you.

Beam deflectors need to be fitted to your headlights. This is very cheap and straightforward, but it has to be done or else your headlights will dip to the centre of the road. In fact some models of cars have an internal switch that will do the same job. You will need to display an IRL plate at the rear of the car and you should also be carrying a First Aid kit.

A warning triangle is compulsory in most countries and is strongly recommended even when not legally required.

TEST YOUR UNDERSTANDING OF THIS SECTION

1. Why should you try to yield to farm vehicles on a narrow road?
2. What precautions should you take when setting out to drive for a long distance on your own?
3. If you break down on a motorway, why are you advised to get out of the car?
4. What is an IDP and where would you get one?
5. Why should you notify your insurance company if you are taking your car abroad?
6. If taking your car to the Continent, what adjustment do you need to make to your head lights?
7. Name the three EU countries where you drive on the left.
8. Is Ireland's drink drive limit higher or lower than the European norm?

ANSWERS ON PAGE 174

CHAPTER 4

ANSWERS

CHAPTER 1

Answers to questions on 'Get into the car…'

1. The main blind spot is over your right shoulder, but remember that this is not the only blind spot.
2. You should stop immediately if your oil warning light comes on. If you continue driving you will damage the engine.
3. You should check all the following regularly: the levels of oil and radiator coolant, the tyre pressures, the windscreen wipers and washers, all the front and rear lights (including number plate lights) and indicators, and the horn.
4. You check the oil by pulling out the dipstick and wiping it with a clean cloth; then return it to its place and pull out again, and look at the level showing between the markers. Don't forget: for an accurate reading, the car should be on a level road surface, and the engine cool.
5. The legally required tread depth is at least 1.6mm all round the tyre, and for three-quarters of the width across the centre of the tyre.

Answers to questions on 'Can you handle it?'

1. Before you start the engine, check that the gear lever is in neutral and the handbrake on.
2. MSMM stands for Mirror, Signal, Mirror, Manoeuvre. This is the sequence you should follow before moving off, making a turn etc. Look in your rear view mirror –

indicate, if necessary and if the way is clear – check over your shoulder (the blind spot) – and then move in the chosen direction.
3. There is almost always a blind spot somewhere in the driver's field of vision, so take a quick glance over your shoulder as well as checking the mirrors.
4. Yes, but not the other way around. If you take the test in an automatic then you are only licensed to drive an automatic.
5. Start the car with the gear lever in 'Park' or 'Neutral', put your foot on the brake pedal, then select 'Drive' and smoothly release the brake. This may cause the car to start moving forward.

Answers to questions on 'Are you legal?'

1. A provisional licence.
2. You must get at least 35 out of 40 questions correct.
3. National Car Test.
4. A Category B licence covers driving 'ordinary' cars up to 3.5 tonnes in weight.
5. Learner drivers are not allowed to use motorways.

Answers to questions on 'Who's in charge?'

1. You should look for an instructor who is fully qualified and a professional. You could try asking advice from friends who have recently learned to drive.
2. At the moment there are no official standards that driving instructors are required to meet. However that is likely to change soon, as a registration scheme is to be introduced.
3. No. You must be supervised by a fully licensed driver.
4. All cars must display a tax disc, an

insurance disc and if a car is more than four years old, an NCT certificate.

5. Is the car modern? Is it reliable? Is it insured?

Answers to questions on 'Look after your car…'

1. You should get your car serviced regularly to keep it in good condition. If you do not you are more likely to have a breakdown, more likely to face an expensive repair bill and more likely to fail the NCT. A full service history also maintains the car's resale value.
2. Rear fog lights are very powerful, and in clear conditions they can dazzle the car behind.
3. Because it is poisonous. Also because the braking system is – obviously – critical for safety and has to be maintained very carefully.
4. Power-assisted steering takes much of the hard work out of manoeuvring the car, and makes parking in tight spaces easier. Sometimes, however, if you lock the steering round too hard you may stall the car. Do not turn the steering wheel while the car is stationary.
5. In bad weather your windscreen rapidly becomes covered in spray from the vehicle in front, and you will not be able to see clearly to drive safely unless you can clear the screen at regular intervals. The problem is made worse when there is a low sun ahead.
6. Yes, although unless they are children the legal responsibility is theirs, not yours. Where there are rear seat belts available in the car, your passengers must wear them.
7. Catalytic converters are fitted in exhaust systems to make the emissions less harmful to the environment. Levels of carbon monoxide and hydrocarbons emitted are measured as part of the NCT test; the allowable levels are being tightened up further for newer cars.

8. When you arrive at the garage, you should switch off your engine and extinguish cigarettes. Do not use mobile phones.
9. You know the tank is full when the automatic cut-out operates. Do not attempt to put more fuel in after this point.
10. You can demonstrate your commitment to helping the environment by having regular services and keeping the engine tuned, checking tyre pressures, driving without harsh acceleration or at excessive speeds, and by not carrying unnecessary weight such as an empty roof rack. Plan your journeys to avoid congestion whenever possible, using route planners and heeding advice from organisations such as AA Roadwatch. You can also consider choosing a car capable of running on biofuels.

CHAPTER 2

Answers to questions on 'Motorists with attitude'

1. Physically, young people are usually faster. But remember that you need judgement as well as speed. Research has shown that young drivers tend to over-estimate their ability to anticipate and respond to hazards on the road. After about three years' experience it improves. Age is less important than experience.
2. There is no one 'right' speed – you should drive at or slightly below the speed limit for the road you are on. Be prepared to drive more slowly in built-up areas.

CHAPTER 5

3. Research suggests that 95% of crashes are caused by human error.

4. 'Coasting' is unsafe because it reduces your control of the steering, which could lead to an accident.

5. 'Only a fool breaks the two second rule' is a good line to memorise; it refers to keeping at least a two-second gap between your vehicle and the one in front and takes about two seconds to recite. However, you should double this gap in rain, and increase it ten times in icy conditions.

Answers to questions on 'I didn't even see him...'

1. Among the skills you need to be a safe driver are: anticipation, observation, concentration and forward planning. It may help if you memorise OAP – Observe, Anticipate, Plan.

2. Any of the following can cause you to stop concentrating fully on the road: the behaviour of pedestrians or passengers; roadside advertising; too much information to process all at once; and using mobile phones. In addition, if you've got something on your mind, you may start worrying about that problem and forget to give your full attention to your driving.

3. You should find a safe place to stop before making the call. It's not safe to carry on driving while using a mobile phone.

4. Six hours is too long to drive without a break; make a couple of rest stops on the way and you will feel better and improve your ability to concentrate. Don't just pull into a garage – get out at a safe place and walk around. And don't be tempted to speed up so as to get to the rest area more quickly – open the window to let in some fresh air.

5. In icy conditions, allow at least ten times the space you would usually allow between you and the car in front. Drive more slowly so that you won't skid if you have to brake. Use the technique of progressive braking. The road conditions can change unexpectedly and you may hit a patch of black ice. And, if you can avoid making the journey, don't drive in icy weather.

Answers to questions on 'It's in the rules'

1. When two vehicles are approaching an unmarked junction from different directions, neither has priority. Use great caution as you cross, making use of 'right-left-right' observation.

2. You are allowed to enter a box junction before your exit is clear if you are turning right and you are only prevented (temporarily) by oncoming traffic.

3. You should wait until the car on the right has actually begun to turn; the driver might suddenly change his or her mind and go straight on, or they might have their left indicator on in error.

4. A long, narrow 'upside-down' triangle marked on the road warns you that there is a 'Yield' junction just ahead.

5. If it will not impede the flow of following traffic, you can move into the correct lane by using 'Mirror, Signal, Mirror, Manoeuvre'. But if you can see it's not safe to do so, you will have to stay in the wrong lane and find another route to your destination.

6. The key rule at roundabouts is 'Give way to traffic from the right'.

7. If the traffic sign marking a cycle lane has times of operation shown, you are allowed to use the lane outside those times.

8. Legally you are not required to stop if the

pedestrian has not yet set foot on the crossing, but it is far better to get into the habit of slowing down and anticipating that a pedestrian may be waiting to cross, and then allowing them plenty of time to do so.

9. The three main types of sign are Regulatory, Warning and Information.

10. A solid white line means that you must stay to the left and may not cross the line (unless it is for access or in an emergency).

11. Street lights usually indicate a speed limit of 50kph or 60kph.

12. National Primary Roads usually have a speed limit of 100kph unless a different limit is marked. The usual speed limit for motorways is 120kph.

13. Reaction time may vary depending on how alert you are, how well you're concentrating and even how recently you have eaten.

14. Although an aspect of good driving skills is 'making normal progress', this does not mean that you should drive at the maximum allowed by the speed limit if the weather is bad; at night; on bends; or when driving a large vehicle. You should always adjust your speed to the conditions.

15. Progressive braking means gentle braking in good time to slow the car gradually.

Answers to questions on 'You can't park there!'

1. Park as close to the kerb as possible, with your wheels parallel to it. Avoid parking with your wheels half-on and half-off the kerb.

2. In town centres, make use of car parks, meter zones and 'park-and-ride' schemes. In towns, rectangular signs with a white letter 'P' on a blue background guide you to the car parks.

3. No. You may not park in a 'Disabled' space (one reserved for a driver with disabilities)

at any time. Nor are you allowed to do so if you remain with your car.

4. Opening your door could be a hazard to oncoming traffic, for example by forcing a cyclist or motorcyclist to swerve.

5. Bad parking can be dangerous if you block sightlines for other traffic or for pedestrians.

Answers to questions on 'Driving under the influence'

1. Approximately 30,000. Gardai no longer need to have formed an opinion that alcohol has been consumed before requesting a breath sample. Once a check point has been set up, any driver may be asked to provide one.

2. Don't drink any alcohol. 'How to avoid being caught' is an example of asking the wrong sort of question. Ensure that the evening is both safe and enjoyable for all concerned by agreeing on someone who won't drink alcohol that evening to be the driver. Or, you could use public transport or taxis.

3. If you drink alcohol in the evening it's quite possible that you will still be over the limit the following morning; this will almost certainly be the case if you drink heavily.

4. Your coordination, reaction speed and hazard awareness will all be affected, as well as your ability to judge distance and speed. You may well feel over-confident about your skill as a driver and take more risks than normal, posing a danger to yourself, to other drivers and pedestrians. Remember: drinking and night driving often go together, and it's more difficult to spot hazards in the dark.

5. The law is very similar for drug driving. It is an offence to drive a car while impaired; the punishments are the same no matter what substance is causing the impairment.

Answers to questions on 'It's different at night'

1. You should take even more care when driving at night because hazards are more difficult to see in the dark; pedestrians are more difficult to see, and may be less predictable in their behaviour.
2. Dipped headlights are used at all times at night except: on restricted roads with a speed limit of 50kph or less and where street lamps are not more than 185 metres (600 feet) apart; on roads with no street lights when you could dazzle vehicles ahead; and in the daytime in dull or rainy conditions.
3. Generally you would not expect to use full beam headlights on a motorway, unless you are on an unlit section and you are not driving in a stream of traffic.
4. Fog lights should only be used in fog or poor visibility; you should switch them off again as soon as you can see clearly.
5. Your knowledge of the traffic ahead can sometimes be improved at night because you can see oncoming vehicles by their headlights – sometimes before they have rounded a corner ahead of you. However, your peripheral vision is reduced to what you can see from the beams of your own headlights.

Answers to questions on 'Stormy weather'

1. You should double the time you allow for braking and stopping when driving on a wet road. For driving on ice, allow as much as ten times the normal stopping distance.
2. If you find your car has gone into a skid, ease off the brake or accelerator and steer smoothly in the same direction as the skid. If your car has anti-lock brakes it may be possible to continue braking firmly while you steer out of the skid.
3. First decide whether your journey is really necessary; if it is, clear all snow and ice from the vehicle and demist the windscreen thoroughly before you start out. Carry food, drink, warm clothes and boots or stout shoes in case of emergencies, as well as a spade for digging the car out of drifts.
4. No. In fog drivers can quickly become disorientated, and may start to follow closely behind the rear lights of the car in front as it makes them feel more secure. This can be dangerous, as you need to have enough space to stop suddenly. If you have to slow down yourself, use your mirror first and brake slowly if possible, as other cars may be following too closely behind you for the reason given above.
5. As soon as you have driven out of fog, switch off your rear fog lights, as they are too bright for normal use and will dazzle other drivers. The use of rear fog lights can have the effect of preventing your brake lights being visible.

Answers to questions on 'Motorway rules'

1. Learner drivers are not allowed on motorways; along with motor cycles under 50cc, tractors, horse riders, cyclists and pedestrians. But learners can observe how motorway driving is different from other driving when they are passengers in someone else's car. Immediately after passing the test it's a good idea to have at least one motorway lesson with your instructor. Driving on dual carriageways can provide a similar experience.
2. Before starting a long motorway journey

carry out all the standard checks on your car; driving at high speed for long distances can increase the risk of breakdowns, and motorway tailbacks can make engine overheating more likely.

3. You should join the motorway by building up your speed to fit in with the flow of traffic in the left lane; indicating right; and then moving across when there is a space or someone moves to the centre lane to let you in. Give way to traffic already on the motorway rather than speeding up to cut in. Once you have joined, stay in the left lane so that you can adjust to the higher driving speed. Show the same courtesy to other drivers joining the motorway.

4. 120kph is the usual speed, although sometimes lower speed limits are applied, for example when there are roadworks.

5. There are no times when you should overtake on the left, but you are allowed to keep up with traffic in a lane which happens to be moving faster than the lane to the right for a period of time. This may happen when all traffic in the left lane is leaving the motorway at the next exit, but both lanes to the right are filled with slow-moving traffic.

6. Vehicles incapable of travelling at at least 50kph are not allowed to use motorways.

7. Motorway signs are blue with white letters or symbols.

8. You use the outside lane for overtaking, or to allow traffic to join from a slip road on the left. You do not cruise in the outside lane.

9. HGV, trucks and buses are not allowed to use the outside lane and nor are cars that are towing trailers.

10. You may not stop on the hard shoulder unless you have broken down; it should not be used by anyone who feels like a

cigarette, to swap drivers or because children say they can't wait till the service area. If you break down, stop as far to the left as possible, switch on your hazard warning lights, and get everyone out of the vehicle and well away from the motorway (animals should be left in the vehicle). Contact the Gardai via the emergency phone; the markers indicate the direction of the nearest one. If you are unable to get your vehicle off the carriageway and on to the hard shoulder, switch on hazard warning lights and leave the vehicle only when safe. Do not put a warning triangle on the motorway.

CHAPTER 3

Answers to questions on 'How am I driving?'

1. Drivers arriving from countries where they drive on the right are at risk of being disorientated when they drive off the ferry, or drive away from the airport. Keep at a safe distance and don't sound your horn or flash your lights at the driver, as he or she may be tired from travel and struggling to cope with unfamiliar road signs.

2. Arm signals are used infrequently by car drivers but are used all the time by horse riders, cyclists etc. As a car driver you need to be completely familiar with the signals used by these other road users. Use arm signals when necessary to reinforce indicator signals. A full list of arm signals is given in the Rules of the Road, including those for letting anyone controlling traffic know your intentions.

3. The Gardai will direct you to pull over by using flashing blue lights and left indicators.

Check that it is safe to pull over, then stop and switch off your engine. Remember to have the legally required documents to hand; any that you are not carrying with you may be produced at a Garda station within seven days.

4. The horn has a specific purpose – it is to warn other road users of your presence or of an emergency. Using it to 'express your opinion' is illegal. It may also provoke an angry response if the other motorist has a short fuse!

5. You should always anticipate bends, and any other potential hazard, by slowing down in a controlled manner so that you can steer round the bend at a safe speed. Brake as you approach the bend, then start to apply the accelerator gently while in the bend. If you are driving too fast round the bend you are likely to cross the centre line and cause a hazard to oncoming drivers.

Answers to questions on 'I'm right behind you!'

1. Tailgating means driving too close behind another vehicle, often with an intent to intimidate or harass the driver. It is dangerous because if you are too close you will not have enough room to stop in an emergency, especially if the road is wet or icy. If you get too close behind a large vehicle you will not be able to see the road ahead well enough to overtake that vehicle safely.

2. Flashing your headlights could intimidate the other driver and cause them to lose concentration, thus making accidents more likely to happen. Using full beam headlights when driving behind another car will produce a dazzling glare in their rear view mirror which is dangerous. The technique of driving very close and flashing headlights is often used by impatient drivers on a motorway when they wish to dislodge someone they consider too slow from the centre or right lane; at motorway speeds, this is also a dangerous practice.

3. Hazard warning lights are intended for use when the car is stationary and causing an obstruction. They should not be used while driving, except for short periods on a motorway or unrestricted dual carriageway, to warn other drivers of a hazard ahead.

4. You should sound your horn only in emergencies, or to let other road users know you are there.

5. Normally you should never sound the horn when your car is stationary, but you are allowed to do so in order to prevent an accident if you see a vehicle approaching which is likely to put you in danger.

Answers to questions on 'It's not me, it's the others!'

1. You should move to the left and allow the driver to complete their manoeuvre safely. It is not your function to police the other driver's behaviour, and safety is everyone's objective.

2. Although a truck driver may use flashing left indicators as a signal that it is safe for you to overtake, you should only do so when you can see clearly that the road ahead is clear and that there is plenty of room to complete the manoeuvre. Drivers of slow vehicles should pull over and stop to let traffic pass when they find a safe place to do so.

3. In wet weather you should double the 'two second rule' about how long it takes to stop, and in icy conditions you need to multiply the time of two seconds by ten.

4. You should allow at least as much room when overtaking a motorcyclist – a car's width – as you would for a car, because the motorcyclist may swerve, or be blown towards you by high winds.

5. Once you are sure it is safe to overtake, you should proceed confidently, get past the other vehicle and return to your normal position without 'cutting in'. If you begin an overtaking manoeuvre and then hesitate or lose your nerve, you could be a hazard to other drivers.

Answers to questions on 'Who goes first?'

1. That the pedestrian is elderly is not the most important factor here. If the pedestrian is waiting on the pavement, you can continue round the corner if it would be unsafe to do otherwise because of following traffic, but if you can safely slow down and let the pedestrian cross first, then do so. If, on the other hand, the pedestrian is already crossing the side road, then he or she has priority. But remember: don't wave anyone across.

2. Always give way to trams – they cannot steer to avoid you. Do not attempt to overtake them, especially on the inside if they have stopped to pick up passengers at a tram stop in the centre of the road. Get to know the signs that are meant just for tram drivers.

3. Give way to cyclists in cycle lanes and on toucan crossings. Stay well back from a cyclist who has indicated that he or she wishes to change lanes, or when you are approaching a junction or roundabout behind a cyclist.

4. Horse riders are permitted to ride two abreast, though they must drop back to single file on narrow roads or when approaching a bend. The outer of the two riders may be shielding a younger or less experienced person.

5. You should stop and switch off your engine when asked to do so by someone in charge of farm animals. (After all, there is little point in doing anything else!)

6. A long vehicle will pull out to the right in preparation for turning left (although it would be incorrect to do so in a car). Slow down and give way to the long vehicle.

7. You should wait until your view of the major road is completely clear before pulling out. Your view will be obscured until the vehicle has finished turning into the side road.

8. Use your mirrors to anticipate the ambulance's path through the traffic, then pull over and slow down or pause if it is safe to do so.

9. You must obey the Garda. A signal from the Garda overrides all other traffic signals.

10. Flashing blue beacons are used only by the emergency services.

Answers to questions on 'Road users at risk'

1. Cyclists and motorcyclists are more vulnerable than car drivers because they have little protection, they can be blown off course by strong winds, and they are often riding outside the car driver's field of vision. An object as thin as a lamppost can obscure your view of a motorcyclist.

2. Be on the look-out for children in residential areas, on their way to or from school, or playing in the street. Be aware that they do not always realise the danger from cars, and may run out into the street unexpectedly.

3. The white cane means that the person is

ANSWERS

visually impaired. The red band indicates that they are also hard of hearing.

4. Passive safety systems like airbags have significantly improved passenger protection. However, protection for vulnerable road users like cyclists and pedestrians has not improved as much.

5. A pedestrian hit by a car travelling at 60kph is likely to be killed. Every kph by which you reduce your speed in built-up areas reduces the likelihood of your inflicting serious injury on another person in the event of an accident.

Answers to questions on 'Shift that load!'

1. When towing a caravan or trailer you have to allow for the effect of the extra length and weight when you are manoeuvring, turning or parking. You will need to show even more care and concentration than usual, as well as an awareness of other road users.

2. 'Snaking' is the word used to describe what happens when a caravan being towed at too high a speed begins to swerve out of control. This may also happen as a result of high winds. The driver must ease off the accelerator and brake gently while regaining control of the steering. Always observe the appropriate speed limit, which for cars towing trailers is never more than 80kph.

3. The weight should be distributed as evenly as possible, to minimise the risk of losing control. The load should be safely secured and should not stick out in a dangerous manner.

4. No! Passengers are not allowed to ride in a trailer while it is on tow, so you cannot use your caravan as additional seating for people travelling with you. All passengers

must ride inside the car and wear seatbelts.

5. A roof rack will affect the aerodynamic performance of your vehicle. This will reduce fuel efficiency and will make the vehicle more vulnerable to crosswinds.

Answers to questions on 'It's your responsibility'

1. Not as far as seat restraints are concerned: that's your responsibility. The driver will have penalty points applied to their licence if they fail to ensure that all children under 17 years of age are wearing seat belts.

2. Appropriate restraints include child seats, harnesses and baby seats of approved design. For very small children a booster seat suitable for their weight can be positioned on the back seat.

3. A child may require a booster seat up until 12 years of age, unless their height exceeds 1.5 metres.

4. It is not safe because the forces involved in a crash would easily rip the child from the adult's arms.

5. A rear-facing baby seat should never be positioned in a front seat that has an air-bag installed, because the explosive force of the airbag may strike the back of the babyseat and that impact could harm the baby.

Answers to questions on 'Trust me, I'm a first-aider'

1. Bandages, plasters, safety-pins, scissors, sterile dressings, antiseptic wipes, disposable gloves. A ready-assembled First Aid kit should contain these items.

2. There is a high risk of fire at an accident scene, and any spilt fuel could be ignited by a spark from a cigarette.

3. When calling the emergency services, be ready to give the location of the accident as

fully as you can, and say how many vehicles are involved and how many people are injured.

4. You should not move casualties unless you know there is an immediate danger of fire or explosion.

5. ABC stands for Airway, Breathing, Circulation. This is a good way to remember the First Aid procedure.

6. Do not give an accident victim anything to eat or drink.

7. Continue on your way without causing a delay by slowing down to look. Once the professionals are on the scene, let them handle it.

8. You should provide your name and address, and that of the vehicle's owner if different, to anyone at an accident scene with reasonable grounds for requesting them.

9. If Gardai do not attend at the accident scene you have 24 hours in which to report the accident to them; but you should not wait that long unless you have any good reason, but rather report it as quickly as possible.

10. No, you should not. There is a very serious risk of a neck injury when a motorcyclist crashes, and attempting to remove the helmet is likely to make this worse.

CHAPTER 4

Answers to questions on 'Applying for your test'

1 The test costs €38.

2. There are 49 test centres, five of them in Dublin.

3. It is best to spend your time on the waiting list learning properly and building up your experience.

4. The disadvantages are that many drivers will have picked up bad habits and forgotten correct procedure.

5. The overall pass rate for the test is approximately 55%.

Answers to questions on 'What happens on the day?'

1. The tester will check your provisional licence, and will also ask you to sign a form that says that your car is roadworthy and that you are insured to drive it.

2. The tester will ask you to recognise pictures of regulatory and warning signs.

3. You will be asked to demonstrate at least three technical checks.

4. This means that you are not travelling so slowly as to be a hazard or a frustration to traffic behind you.

5. There are two. Reversing around a corner, and reversing as part of the 'turnabout'.

6. The tester will be assessing whether you are competent at controlling the car, how you react to any hazards, and whether you are noticing and reacting correctly to traffic signs and signals.

7. Nobody is perfect! You can make up to nine Grade 2 faults overall and still pass the test. Grade 1 faults do not affect the result.

8. You should not have to encroach on the approach lane for drivers on the other road.

9. Any Grade 3 'dangerous or potentially dangerous' fault means a test failure.

10. The test lasts for between 40 and 45 minutes.

Answers to questions on 'Passed?'

1. The tester will hand you a 'Certificate of Competency'.
2. You can drive a vehicle up to 3.5 tonnes.
3. It is still useful to know where your weaknesses lie and to work on them.
4. Once a driver reaches 70 years of age they can only apply for a three year licence.
5. No! Statistics show that drivers remain high risk before building up experience, but you are obviously doing well so far!

Answers to questions on 'Advanced driving skills – who needs them?'

1. Because there is no requirement for any qualification after passing the test, people tend to see that as the 'end' of their driver's education.
2. By taking an advanced driver course and by consciously remembering what you have been taught when you were a 'learner'.
3. You can find out about advanced driving courses from the Institute of Advanced Motoring or from the AA.
4. You should tell someone where you are going and when you expect to arrive. Also you should carry a mobile phone so that you can call for help in the case of a breakdown or an emergency.

Answers to questions on 'Buying your first car'

1. Do you need a manual or automatic car? Do you need to tow a trailer? What type of roads will you be driving on most frequently and how many passengers are you likely to need to carry?
2. Second-hand cars can be good value because the value of new cars depreciates so rapidly.
3. The cost of insurance, servicing, maintenance, fuel and repairs and replacements, for example, tyres.
4. The SIMI operates an arbitration scheme to deal with complaints.

Answers to questions on 'Alone at last'

1. Farm vehicles are more difficult to manoeuvre than a car, so it makes sense for you to be the one to yield.
2. You should let someone know where you are going and roughly when you expect to arrive. Also, you should carry a mobile phone!
3. The risk of an accident on the hard shoulder is greater than the risk to your safety from strangers, since there are (usually) no pedestrians on a motorway.
4. An International Driving Permit, issued by the AA.
5. If you do not notify your insurer then you will only be given the legal minimum level of cover in whatever country you are driving in.
6. You need to fit beam deflectors to stop your dipped head lights pointing towards the centre of the road.
7. Ireland, the UK and Malta.
8. At 80 milligrammes, it's the highest. 50 milligrammes is the norm and some limits are even lower.

No. 000000

DRIVING TEST REPORT

1. Passed your Driving Test

Having passed your driving test you should nevertheless continue to pay particular attention to the faults marked overleaf without neglecting other aspects of your driving.

2. Failure of your Driving Test

Failure of the test arises where you incur any of the following:

1 or more grade 3 faults;

4 of the same grade 2 faults for a single aspect;

6 or more grade 2 faults under the same heading; or a total of

9 or more grade 2 faults overall.

Up to a maximum of 4 grade 2 faults may be recorded for any single aspect.

3. Grading of faults

Faults are graded as follows:

Grade 1 (Green Area) Minor Fault, Grade 2 (Blue Area) More Serious Fault, Grade 3 (Pink Area) Dangerous/Potentially Dangerous faults or total disregard of traffic controls.

Grade 1 faults do not affect the rest result.

A combination of 3 or more unanswered or incorrectly answered questions on the Rules of the Road/ Checks, constitutes a grade 2 fault. (Checks include doors closed safely, the headrest, mirrors, seat and seat-belt adjustments, and for motorcyclists, the helmet, gloves, boots and protective clothing).

3 or more hand signals not demonstrated correctly constitutes a grade 2 fault.

3 or more Secondary Controls not demonstrated correctly constitutes a grade 2 fault. (Secondary controls include temperature controls, fan, air vents, rear-window heater, wipers, windscreen washer, light switches, air intake control, rear fog light and air conditioner, if fitted).

Not operating a Secondary Control as required during the practical test can also constitute a fault.

4. Technical Checks — all categories

Inability to describe a check on 3 or more of the following constitutes a grade 2 fault:

The tyres, lights, reflectors, indicators, engine oil, coolant, windscreen washer fluid, steering, brakes and horn. Where necessary, the bonnet should be opened and closed safely. For motorcyclists the checks can also include the chain, and the emergency stop-switch, if fitted.

For categories C1, C, D1, D, EC1, ED1, and ED technical checks include the following as appropriate to the category:

The power assisted braking and steering systems, the condition of the wheels, wheel nuts, mudguards, windscreen, windows, wipers, air-pressure, air tanks, suspension, engine oil, coolant, windscreen washer fluid, the loading mechanism if fitted, the body, sheets, cargo doors, cabin locking, way of loading and securing the load, and checking and using the instrument panel and tachograph.

For categories D1, D, ED1 and ED technical checks include controlling the body, service doors, emergency exits, first aid equipment, fire extinguishers and other safety equipment.

5. Coupling/Uncoupling includes

a) Checking the coupling mechanism and the brake and electrical connections,

b) Uncoupling and recoupling the trailer from/to its towing vehicle using the correct sequence. The towing vehicle must be parked alongside the trailer as part of the exercise.

Parking in relation to categories EB, C1, C, EC1, and EC includes parking safely at a ramp or platform for loading/unloading.

Parking in relation to D1, D, ED1, and ED includes parking safely to let passengers on or off the bus.

6. Motorcyclists

Safety glance means looking around to check blind spots as necessary.

7. Preparing for your next Driving Test

In Preparing for your next test you should pay particular attention to the items which have been marked. Further information on these and other aspects of the test are contained in the booklet entitled "Rules of the Road" which is available at book shops and in the leaflet "Preparing for your Driving Test" which is issued with the acknowledgement of your application.

8. Note

Items on which faults occurred during your driving test are marked overleaf. The driver tester is not permitted to discuss the details of the test.

Údarás Um Shábháilteacht Ar Bhóithre
Road Safety Authority

Oifigí Rialtais, Béal an Átha, Co. Mhaigh Eo / Government Offices, Ballina, Co. Mayo.
locall: 1890 40 60 40 fax: (096) 78 287 website: www.drivingtest.ie

CHAPTER 5

DRIVING TEST REPORT

NAME OF APPLICANT:

DATE: DAY MONTH YEAR   REG. NO.

FAULTS	GRADE 1	GRADE 2	GRADE 3
1. RULES/CHECKS			
2. POSITION VEHICLE CORRECTLY AND IN GOOD TIME			
ON THE STRAIGHT			
ON BENDS			
IN TRAFFIC LANES			
AT CROSS JUNCTIONS			
AT ROUNDABOUTS			
TURNING RIGHT			
TURNING LEFT			
STOPPING			
FOLLOWING TRAFFIC			
3. TAKE PROPER OBSERVATION			
MOVING OFF			
OVERTAKING			
CHANGING LANES			
AT CROSS JUNCTIONS			
AT ROUNDABOUTS			
TURNING RIGHT			
TURNING LEFT			
4. REACT PROMPTLY AND PROPERLY TO HAZARDS			
REACTION			
5. USE MIRRORS PROPERLY, IN GOOD TIME AND BEFORE SIGNALLING			
MOVING OFF			
ON THE STRAIGHT			
OVERTAKING			
CHANGING LANES			
AT ROUNDABOUTS			
TURNING RIGHT			
TURNING LEFT			
SLOWING/STOPING			
6. ALLOW SUFFIENT CLEARANCE TO			
PEDESTRIANS			
CYCLISTS			
STATIONARY VEHICLES			
OTHER TRAFFIC			
OTHER OBJECTS			
OVERTAKE SAFELY			
7. GIVE CORRECT SIGNALS IN GOOD TIME			
MOVING OFF			
OVERTAKING			
CHANGING LANES			
AT ROUNDABOUTS			
TURNING RIGHT			
TURNING LEFT			
STOPPING			
CANCEL PROMPTLY			
HAND SIGNALS			
BECKONING OTHERS			
MISLEADING			
8. MOTORCYCLES			
SAFETY GLANCE			
U-TURN: CONTROL/OBS.			
SLOW RIDE			
PARK ON/OFF STAND			
WALK ALONGSIDE			
9. COURTESY			
10. ALIGHTING			

FAULTS	GRADE 1	GRADE 2	GRADE 3
11. MAINTAIN REASONABLE PROGRESS AND AVOID UNDUE HESITANCY WHEN			
MOVING OFF			
ON THE STRAIGHT			
OVERTAKING			
AT CROSS JUNCTIONS			
AT ROUNDABOUTS			
TURNING RIGHT			
TURNING LEFT			
CHANGING LANES			
AT TRAFFIC LIGHTS			
12. MAKE PROPPER USE OF VEHICLE CONTROLS			
ACCELERATOR			
CLUTCH			
GEARS			
FOOTBRAKE			
HANDBRAKE			
STEERING			
SECONDARY CONTROLS			
TECHNICAL CHECKS			
COUPLING/UNCOUPLING			
13. ADJUST SPEED TO SUIT/ON APPROACH			
ROAD CONDITIONS			
TRAFFIC CONDITIONS			
ROUNDABOUTS			
CROSS JUNCTIONS			
TURNING RIGHT			
TURNING LEFT			
TRAFFIC CONTROLS			
SPEED LIMIT			
14. COMPLY WITH TRAFFIC CONTROLS			
TRAFFIC LIGHTS			
TRAFFIC SIGNS			
ROAD MARKINGS			
PEDESTRIAN CROSSING			
GARDA/SCHOOL WARDEN			
BUS LANES			
CYCLE LANES			
15. YIELD RIGHT OF WAY AS REQUIRED			
MOVING OFF			
OVERTAKING			
CHANGING LANES			
AT JUNCTIONS			
AT ROUNDABOUTS			
TURNING RIGHT			
TURNING LEFT			
16. REVERSE			
COMPETENTLY			
OBSERVATION			
RIGHT OF WAY			
17. TURNABOUT			
COMPETENTLY			
OBSERVATION			
RIGHT OF WAY			
18. PARKING, LOADING/UNLOADING/PASSENGER STOPS			
COMPETENTLY			
OBSERVATION			
RIGHT OF WAY			